"Sobriety is absolutely a pathway of spiritual awakening. I'm so grateful to Erin Jean Warde for this necessary and hopeful book on the joy that can be found in a sober spirituality. You are in good hands here. As she shows us, a mindful relationship with alcohol is a beautiful part of how we evolve into the freedom of being fully awake and alive. What a healing gift to the church!"

—**Sarah Bessey**, editor of the *New York Times* bestseller
A Rhythm of Prayer and author of *Jesus Feminist*

"Erin Jean Warde writes a poetic, tender, and spiritual book grounded in the kind of compassion that is born of deep love. Intersectional and bold, *Sober Spirituality* weaves personal narrative with research and Scripture. *Sober Spirituality* is a gentle invitation to explore the divinity within us."

—**Beverly Gooden**, author of *Surviving: Why We Stay* and
How We Leave Abusive Relationships

"What a balm this book is! And not just for those acquainted with addiction (but for them too). My friend Erin Jean Warde offers hard-won wisdom and precious pastoral guidance to anyone in need of tangible hope to get through the day. *Sober Spirituality* is a beautiful and vital reminder that while our belovedness doesn't begin when we are in recovery, the grace of God can sustain us in that journey, come what may."

—**David Zahl**, author of *Low Anthropology* and
director of Mockingbird Ministries

"My favorite spiritual writing reveals the sacramental nature of all of life, which is exactly what Erin Jean Warde does in *Sober Spirituality*. She stands humbly yet boldly within the contemplative and mystic traditions, offering words that

illuminate the integration of body, mind, and soul within the life of faith. With accessible language, transparent storytelling, and midrashic scriptural interpretation, Warde offers a courageous tenderness to the reader and a loving challenge to the church, identifying areas of our complicity in propping up a culture that prevents people from approaching relationships with alcohol mindfully."

—**Terry J. Stokes**, pastor and author of *Prayers for the People*

"This book speaks gospel truth—truth that is painful, paradoxical, and beautiful. Both soulful and practical, *Sober Spirituality* is a trustworthy guide for those who are sober or sober-curious. Erin Jean Warde will make you laugh and then bring you to tears with her honest and courageous truth-telling, grounding you in belovedness every step of the way. An absolute gem of a book from a gem of a human."

—**Danielle Shroyer**, author of *Original Blessing: Putting Sin in Its Rightful Place*

sober
spirituality

THE JOY OF A
MINDFUL RELATIONSHIP
WITH ALCOHOL

ERIN JEAN WARDE

BrazosPress
a division of Baker Publishing Group
Grand Rapids, Michigan

© 2023 by Erin Jean Warde

Published by Brazos Press
a division of Baker Publishing Group
Grand Rapids, Michigan
www.brazospress.com

Printed in the United States of America

Library of Congress Cataloging-in-Publication Data
Names: Warde, Erin Jean, 1987– author.
Title: Sober spirituality : the joy of a mindful relationship with alcohol / Erin Jean Warde.
Description: Grand Rapids, Michigan : Brazos Press, a division of Baker Publishing Group, [2023] | Includes bibliographical references.
Identifiers: LCCN 2022034447 | ISBN 9781587435676 (paperback) | ISBN 9781587436024 (casebound) | ISBN 9781493440504 (ebook) | ISBN 9781493440511 (pdf)
Subjects: LCSH: Addicts—Religious life. | Substance abuse—Religious aspects—Christianity. | Alcohol—Religious aspects—Christianity. | Mindfulness (Psychology)
Classification: LCC BV4596.A24 W37 2023 | DDC 248.8/629—dc23/eng/20221108
LC record available at https://lccn.loc.gov/2022034447

Unless otherwise indicated, Scripture quotations are from the New Revised Standard Version of the Bible, copyright © 1989 National Council of the Churches of Christ in the United States of America. Used by permission. All rights reserved.

Scripture quotations labeled NIV are from THE HOLY BIBLE, NEW INTERNATIONAL VERSION®, NIV® Copyright © 1973, 1978, 1984, 2011 by Biblica, Inc.® Used by permission. All rights reserved worldwide.

Baker Publishing Group publications use paper produced from sustainable forestry practices and post-consumer waste whenever possible.

23   24   25   26   27   28   29   7   6   5   4   3   2   1

For everyone who has chosen to release a life of numbing
in the hope of resurrection.
May you awaken to the Spirit and to yourself.

Joy is what has made the pain bearable
and, in the end, creative rather than destructive.

—Madeleine L'Engle, *A Circle of Quiet*

contents

preface

ONE OF THE MOST gracious realities of sobriety is that it is an always evolving growth process. But grace can sometimes frustrate, so the ever-evolving nature of sobriety is both a gift and a challenge, because it means I'm never quite done, never quite settled. Still, there is joy in the forever journey because it also means I am able to grow inside myself and within the blessing of the Spirit.

This book exists within the gift and challenge of sobriety. It sets out to talk about something that cannot be captured, only explored. *Sober Spirituality* aims not to define sobriety but to foster a heart that is attentive to how our minds, bodies, and souls might be gently asking for a different way of life. This calling to a different way of life might be for you or it might be a calling to a different way of life to bring joy to others. As a reader, this means you will inevitably have different experiences of the book—and thank God! I imagine not everything here will be for you, but I trust the sentiments will each be for someone and that we can celebrate how it will find its way to who it is meant for.

We can sometimes understandably take stigmatized topics very personally, and I encourage us to be aware of this so we can navigate the feeling if it arises. I spend time journeying through truth-telling around alcohol, which includes the difficulty of facing staggering statistics as well as illuminating how the societal norm of promoting alcohol can be harmful. My guess is that parts of this might feel convicting for those of us who have participated in promoting alcohol—an educated guess I can make as someone who is convicted herself.

This book is not written as a finger-wag but as a vessel through which I'm sharing my joy, the wisdom I have received, and my wholeness in mind, body, and soul. But I cannot share the joy and the wholeness without acknowledging where I started. When it came to promoting alcohol use, I was, to share Paul's sentiments, the worst of sinners (1 Tim. 1:15). In this spirit, the inevitable challenge of this work is, from me, confessional, invitational, and offered with a grace that precedes and follows us.

I encourage journeying through this book knowing it is a marathon, not a sprint. I've included "Refresh and Reflect" prompts in each chapter, because even if you don't touch a single reflection question, I hope you will give yourself some time and space as you read. I expect this whole journey—the curiosity, the reckoning with truth, the holy listening to our minds, bodies, and souls—will require silence as much as the wisdom I hope you'll find in these pages.

Sober Spirituality attempts to gather wisdom from all the different areas of my heart and vocation: I am an Episcopal priest, spiritual director, recovery coach, writer, speaker, lover of comedy, Enneagram 6, Twitter super-user, and more. The wisdom gathered reflects books that have put words around what my soul couldn't yet speak, the tender shares from those I have worked with as a recovery coach in both one-on-one and group settings, the outpouring of direct messages I received after I told social media I'm sober (and the DMs I still receive), the holy questions I've held in prayer and penitence with my spiritual directees, different sermons I've preached over the past ten years, and more. I'm not a doctor, therapist, or medical professional, but the depth of honesty I've witnessed through this work is nothing if not a truth-telling about health.

Madeleine L'Engle writes, "Joy is what has made the pain bearable and, in the end, creative rather than destructive."[1] I trust the journey through *Sober Spirituality* will offer you a sense of joy, but the pathway into real joy—the soul's joy—is one of taking a full assessment of our lives. Any honest look into our lives will reveal the pain we have had to face, the moments when we were forced to be at our most vulnerable, and these are the moments when we seek comfort wherever it wills to be found. I offer this book in a spirit of trust that the joy it welcomes will make the pain bearable. Books aside, I believe the joy of a mindful relationship with alcohol helps us withstand moments when we are at our most vulnerable; it is a joy that, if we let it, might usher us into a grace toward ourselves and others that helps us seek out wholeness of mind, body, and soul without hating ourselves in the process. This joy, in all its tumult, promises a life that is creative rather

1. Madeleine L'Engle, *A Circle of Quiet* (New York: HarperOne, 1972), 26.

than destructive. This joy invites us into a death signaling that resurrection is on the way.

May you be tender to yourself, to your pain, to your humanity, to who and how you are in this moment. May you never stray from this tenderness, knowing it is the birthplace of caring for yourself differently. And may you—through this curiosity, compassion, and care—embrace the grace as you weather the frustration that comes along with it, such that you find peace in being never quite done, never quite settled, ever growing in the Spirit.

waking up

An Unexpected Invitation to Joy through Sobriety

TO THIS DAY, I am not a morning person, even as I wake without an alarm by 7 a.m., my body emerging from the grogginess of a trazodone haze and into another day. Before I leave my bed, I will send a good morning tweet of a raccoon meme, even though I know the only way I will meditate is if I meditate before I open Twitter. If you can believe it, this is how I feel now that I love mornings. My mornings are a mixture of coffee, wishing I could go back to bed, and being grateful I have a morning at all: a chance to breathe and a body that no longer awakens to a hangover but to a different type of life. My mornings, even at their worst, feel like perfect wakings after years and years of hangovers. Sobriety redeemed my mornings from hangovers and transformed them into possibility. In the way God resurrected me in sobriety, I am resurrected each day again and again. There is no fear in death because it is destroyed each day when I wake.

The weird thing about hangovers is that I adapted to them. They set the tone for the day: the muscles governing my movement would be sore, the head housing my mind would ache, the seat of my heart would feel broken, and the voices of my soul would speak only shame. I adapted to believing this is how days begin; I came to believe that every day I rested in God, I also had to rest in soreness, ache, heartbroken-ness, and shame. I forgot there was another way. My drinking meant I was shaped to start each day inside a dark night of the soul, even as the rays of sun suggested I could begin again.

When I woke up hung over, mornings were always a marathon.

Oh God, I forgot to get the coffee ready last night.

Wait, when is my first meeting today?

Am I supposed to wear clericals?

Everything was off, everything was more difficult, and—in the chaos of questions—another question couldn't make itself to the front of my heart: Does life have to be this way?

Over time, I began to hide from myself in the mirror. It wasn't intentional, but I'd later realize—after traveling past the mirror seventy billion times to make my crappy coffee—that I always kept my head low. Amid my attempts to never catch my own eyes in the mirror, God caught sight of me each morning and, in the tender gaze of compassion, loved me to the end. It was a love I never lost but also a love I couldn't feel, because if I didn't want to look myself in the eyes, I certainly didn't want to stare into the face of God.

In sobriety, Jesus has seen the part of myself I find most vulnerable, the part of myself I have to work to show, which is of course the heart of myself that is the most true. Alcohol kept the beauty of myself safely hidden out of fear of what might happen if a woman began to believe she had the right to love herself the way God loves her. Alcohol hid me out of fear of what might happen if a woman began to believe that loving herself was not differentiated from her faith but an integral part of it. Shrouded inside everything from gender constructs to vestments to bottomless mimosas, I had been hiding from myself in the mirror because I couldn't look back and see myself anymore.

In sobriety, I started to look into mirrors and see something similar to what God might have had in mind when God gave me breath. I began to wonder if I was still as beloved as I had been before things got so hard, before all the drinking, and if I still retained some of the beauty from the moment when God decided to roll a breath over chaos, willing me to be. I'm still afraid of what loving this part of myself asks of me, because it demands a lot. But it's worth the fear, given what it has brought forth from me, which is nothing less than the abundant life that comes when we let Jesus awaken us to something other than a life of numbness. My life when I was drinking was not the worst life a person could have, but it wasn't abundant, it wasn't joyful, and it wasn't an offering of myself in my beauty and fullness to the world. When I was drinking, I was a breathing tomb, waiting for Christ to destroy my death and resurrect my soul. Now I am an incarnate witness to how the tender healing of God can gently speak into a heart and offer her a life worth living and the awareness that she can trust herself because she is listening with a heart, soul, and mind awakened to God and to herself.

While I was in the first jumbled months of my attempt at sobriety that "stuck," I was drawn into a faith more mystical than concrete, because my sobriety is a mystical experience. I struggled to put words to it as much as I desired to do so. While what was happening could certainly be understood biologically and systematically and practically, the overarching narrative of my sobriety is that something mystical was happening to me. I was, in my choice to quit drinking, experiencing the greatest spiritual awakening I had ever known, and I revel in that continuous awakening to this day.

At the time, I had been ordained, had offered Communion to those with hands open to receive it, had blessed the graves of the faithful, had joined couples in holy matrimony, and had pronounced the forgiveness of God to the penitent—all because I felt called to participate in God's presence on this side of eternity. Yet sobriety stood in front of me as the most beautiful bridge between this world and the next, because it invited me into the mystery of God and myself. I never would have told you I was "drinking away" my life, because I never looked into my glass thinking, "I do not want to feel this and I do not want to be inside my body, so I will drink myself out of this feeling and this body." I lived as a priest with a foot in each world, so numb to both I could barely feel my feet on the earth, could barely notice the divinity begging to be palpable if only I would take the greatest risk by being awake to both worlds, for the greatest reward, living in them the way God wished for me to live.

I got curious about mysticism and fell in love with *Meditations of the Heart* by Howard Thurman. The first paragraph became the cornerstone of my sobriety, the prayer that calls me back into the depths of my decision. Thurman writes:

> There is in every person an inward sea, and in that sea there is an island and on that island there is an altar and standing guard before that altar is the "angel with the flaming sword." Nothing can get by that angel to be placed upon that altar unless it has the mark of your inner authority. Nothing passes "the angel with the flaming sword" to be placed upon your altar unless it be a part of "the fluid area of your consent." This is your crucial link with the Eternal.[1]

Getting sober looked like traversing an inward sea, with sobriety offering me an island, a refuge, a way to get shipwrecked and saved at the same time. The altar here reminds me that even though sobriety has become my greatest healing, I didn't lose the calling to be a woman who lives her life in proximity to holiness, to sacred things, to these altars that gather outward, visible, hurting people like me in order to give us inward graces.

My angel with the flaming sword is my sobriety and I owe my life to it, and to the God who gave me an angel to defend me. The Spirit whispered that I wasn't just worth *something*; I was worth the abundant love of God—a love that I knew I had but that I struggled to receive. From the ordination rite we learn I was called to "nourish Christ's people from the riches of his grace," and I had tried to do that faithfully for many years in the churches I served, but I struggled to let myself be one of Christ's people. I didn't know how to nourish myself from the riches of his grace, and I knew that if I

1. Howard Thurman, *Meditations of the Heart* (Boston: Beacon, 1999), 15.

could receive the riches of his grace through sobriety I would be ever more ready to offer those riches to others. So I began to believe I was worthy of a life lived around the altar on the island inside my inward sea.

When I received an invitation to place bare feet on the hallowed ground of this island, I was ushered into joy—in the most tumultuous understanding of the word. I think joy often sounds like happiness and other fleeting conditions of humanity, but true joy has faithfulness embedded in it to the proverbial bone. During some of the most joyous experiences in the Bible, terror and amazement seize the recipients of good news. There is terror because the news threatens to change them, and there is amazement because of what might be possible if they are changed.

The joy kindled through mindfulness around alcohol invites you into that same terror and amazement. Joy, in its fullest sense, requires truth. If we are joyous because of falsehoods, our joy is incomplete, never leading us into wholeness because it cannot offer us what we ask of it. This is akin to how alcohol never delivers on its promises. Alcohol might promise to relax us, but we wake up sweating in anxiety at 2 a.m. It promises to help us celebrate, but it exacerbates our depression, so we go into a slump when we wish to be exuberant. Alcohol might promise to help us find connection and community, but instead we wake up the morning after a party wondering what we said, fearing that we might have done something to break the very relationships we desire to nourish. Frederick Buechner writes, "The gospel is bad news before it is good news," and this journey shows us a truth that might feel like bad news before we can feel the goodness it provides.[2] In light of the fleeting nature of the promises of alcohol, we can be reconciled to the truth about it and become mindful in the face of that truth, which is good news. Yes, it's the kind of good news that brings us into a joy of equal parts terror and amazement, but this joy is founded on truth. It is a joy with faithfulness embedded to the proverbial bone of your soul, a joy that stands a chance of delivering on its promises.

Thurman proclaims that nothing passes my angel with a flaming sword to be placed upon my altar unless it is by my consent. The consent part was important to me as a woman taught to have almost none, after experiencing my formative years in Deep South fundamentalism. Consent is about believing we are worthy of having agency over ourselves—mind, body, and soul—and knowing we can set those standards without shame, doubt, or caving in on them to please someone else. I wasn't taught how to function inside my agency, or how to set standards and believe I was worthy of holding both myself and others to them. I was passive-aggressively living my whole life—a situation that was only exacerbated by a drug that took me out of the mind, body, and soul I wished to respect. Sobriety allows me to let my *yes* be *yes* and my *no* be *no* so that I honor the people I'm with instead of confusing my *yes* and my *no* in a way that causes resentment. This is yet another way I am becoming more joyful and more true.

We can navigate the fluid area of our consent using one of my least favorite words: mindfulness. Mindfulness is not wallowing; sometimes we need to not be so mindful. We still get to cope, we still get to be indulgent, because there's a

2. Frederick Buechner, *Telling the Truth: The Gospel as Tragedy, Comedy, and Fairy Tale* (New York: HarperCollins, 1977), 7.

difference between assessing your need to zone out for your mental health and numbing as a way of life. Mindfulness is not an invitation to *make peace* with the way things are but the choice to *acknowledge* the way things are. When the news is bad news before it is good news, mindfulness means we tend to it when it's bad news too, not waiting until it becomes good to pay it any mind. We let things be as they are; we let them be with us according to the word of what is real around us and according to where we sit in that reality. Being able to sit in this reality can lead us into a greater reality that we will miss if we rush out of the difficulty: the joy, the moment bad news becomes good news. When we stay in the discomfort that mindfulness provides, we start the journey toward the goodness we are created for, because we journey into the truth that sets us free.

Stewarding my altar, to return to the image from Thurman, is possibly the hardest part of my sober life, because every day I engage with the fluidity Thurman has made me face. He could have used any word—he could have told me it is the *certain* area of my consent, the *secure* area of my consent, the *determined* area of my consent—but he used *fluidity*. Recovery isn't final, it's fluid. But in sobriety, it's not the external tension but the internal tension that gives me the greatest pause. Sure, there is external tension, because, wow, people don't want to talk about sobriety—like, let's absolutely change the topic to something more palatable like religion and politics. Still, external tension cannot rival how the fluid area of my consent brings up extreme inner tension. The fluidity isn't good or bad, it's just real. You can't get sober, you can't resurrect, if you're not ready to be placed fully inside the unknown.

My sobriety is nonnegotiable. There is nothing in my life I will not remove to protect it. My relationships, my vocation, my commitments—they are all honored through my sobriety, and nothing placed in competition with sobriety will win, because there is no competition with resurrection and its irreversible power. My sobriety allows me to love deeply, to receive a joy that will never leave or forsake me. Sobriety allows me to gather myself up and place my soul on the altar, so of course this is my crucial link with the Eternal.

Resurrecting into a joyful life is a profound gift, but it requires that you accept death first, even though you can't possibly know whether this time, somehow, death won't be the end. It is, without question, a leap of faith, because no matter how much I tell you that changing your relationship with alcohol could radically change your life, you will not know whether it is true until you change your relationship with alcohol. Changing your relationship with alcohol means heading into the sea and trusting there is an island on the horizon, an altar to receive your prayers, and an angel to defend you. Changing your relationship with alcohol means trusting that bad news only promises good news is on the way.

refresh and reflect

When you wake up tomorrow, take some time to sit with yourself. Don't be too rigid about it—it doesn't have to be the first thing you do when you wake up—but try to slow down just long enough to see how you feel. How are your muscles, your head, your stomach? How are you talking to yourself, and is it kind or cruel? How do you feel in your soul?

from fundamentalist to whiskeypalian

When Church Is the Hardest Place to Be Sober

I GREW UP NONRELIGIOUS, then got saved at a hell house and joined a Baptist church in Alabama, which led me to fundamentalism (that's a whole other book). When I got to college, I stayed inside the Baptist church but began to wonder whether there was something outside it. I began to do dangerous things, like declaring an English major, which incited me to take an honors composition class with a professor who I would later learn is Episcopalian. This led me down the path I had been told could lead to destruction: reading the Bible as literature. In classes, I felt my mind and heart expand, while church began to feel constrictive. I had more questions than answers and began to believe things I couldn't say in church. However, I had a Baptist college minister who let me wonder and introduced me to some of the books that changed my faith.

While I chose to leave that place of worship, I left with deep grief, because my college minister had loved me through it. He had even given me tools. It's one thing when the Episcopalian English professor tells you that Genesis is poetry; it's another thing entirely when the Baptist campus minister says you might love Brian McLaren. While I wanted to selfishly take that minister with me, I also knew that when we have to go, we have to go, and there's no stopgap on grief.

I took a break from Christianity inside my mind, though I didn't really tell anyone. I wasn't sure what was going on inside me and felt fairly confident the Holy Spirit knew that, so I kept my mouth shut. I wasn't just feeling stifled; I wanted to do things good Baptist girls didn't do. Inside this agnosticism and newfound hedonism, I began to make new friends. When my friend Joseph invited me to a coffee shop Bible study with a priest who didn't recoil when I said I don't believe in hell, I knew my transformation from fundamentalist Christian to Episcopalian was complete. In this new faith context, I discovered that the beliefs I had been ashamed of, the beliefs I had come to believe made me different, could instead be a way for me to unite to others. My doubts didn't have to separate me from the church; they could join me to the Body of Christ. I believed I could be reconciled to my own faith and to the faith of the Church.[1]

1. When I capitalize "Church" by itself, I am referring to the wider church body rather than to specific worship communities.

A buzzword right now is *deconstruction,* which I honor and hold space for as a spiritual director. I deconstructed before Twitter because I am now an elder millennial. It was difficult, but through the Episcopal Church I found a place where I could question, be mad, and lean into mystery. The Book of Common Prayer, coupled with the Bible, provided me with such a beautiful way to conceive of God that I finally felt as though I could be Christian again. To get there I had to come to a primary realization: I was angry at institutions, not God. God has been faithful to me, but institutions are not always faithful to us. I stopped conflating the actions of an institution with the actions of God. I began to worship a liberating God, seeing what I thought was the liberating activity of God in the Episcopal Church, where women are welcome behind the altars and full inclusion of LGBTQ people *is* encouraged—which for an Alabamian former fundamentalist was about as wild and liberating as I could imagine.

The crisis I experienced when I left fundamentalism was similar to the spiritual crisis I entered when I left alcohol behind. Although I have stayed inside the Episcopal Church, where I was introduced to Christians who drink, from early sobriety to now I have wondered whether there is something for me outside it, whether there is a world where my faith is encouraged and my sobriety held as sacred.

For years I wanted to quit, but felt like I couldn't, because I feared that quitting drinking would change my relationships generally but especially within the Episcopal Church—the same way I feared that believing in different things would exclude me from fundamentalist pews. I had been to too many conferences full of Episcopalians where the real community happened over booze; I worried no one would want to connect without the pseudo-communion of drinks at the conference hotel bar. Even before I quit, I began to do dangerous things like reading sobriety blogs. When I got home and dug into those blogs (often after going out for drinks), my mind and heart expanded while my relationship with the Church and my social life began to feel constrictive. Of all the places I never wanted to share questions about my sober curiosity, the Church was at the top of that list. I couldn't imagine Church people knowing I had stopped drinking, so I didn't stop drinking.

My first real attempt at sobriety was the one I thought would work best for a full-time priest: Lent. I wasn't ready to say I was "trying to quit" and hoped a forty-day pious excuse would give me the time to figure it out. Time and again, people reminded me that technically every Sunday is a feast day because it is the Lord's Day, and no one is expected to observe fasts on feast days, so I could still drink one day a week. Even inside the safest excuse to take a sober curious break, I was not free from people encouraging me to drink. From the first attempt, I wasn't supported in my desire to change my relationship with alcohol, especially as a priest. The lack of support culminated in an interior fear that burrowed into my soul: if I quit, I will become an outsider in the Church. This became a roadblock to my recovery.

Alcohol and the Church

One phenomenon I've noticed is the connection between alcohol culture and progressive ideals, including within spiritual communities. Obviously I can't speak to every progressive community, and there are progressive sober spaces, but I'm noticing how often progressive churches define their identity on the basis of who they are not. Many of us left fundamentalism to join a community that felt more connected to social justice. However, we now face a specific binary serving to both denigrate churches and alienate people who are changing their relationship with alcohol: being progressive means you're part of a "drinking church," and conservative fundamentalist churches are for teetotalers. But identities built on who we are not fail to represent our true selves— they're projections.

I can't bring to mind one specific comment, online or off— because there are so many—in which progressive Christians make jokes about how they're "not like those fundamentalists" by somehow illustrating how much they drink or that they drink at church. In a past life, I also made these comments. However, this alienates those of us who have changed our relationship with alcohol, because the inclusivity of the church becomes the exclusivity of the church. Plenty of sober folks are looking for progressive spaces, because some of us have awakened to the social justice concerns around us. The need to identify as a drinking church denigrates us spiritually, because we have let drinking a depressant become a primary identity point. The Church is best known for its belief in the liberating and transformative love of God. Of course, progressive churches with alcohol cultures can be known for the love of God, but this identity marker tempers the impact our spiritual communities could have on the world, because if you hold a pint glass out in front of God as if that's the draw, I won't make it past the beer to meet the God you worship.

Brené Brown says "common enemy intimacy" is a type of relationship built on a foundation of rebelling against what we are not. She writes:

> Common enemy intimacy is counterfeit connection and the opposite of true belonging. If the bond we share with others is simply that we hate the same people, the intimacy we experience is often intense, immediately gratifying, and an easy way to discharge outrage and pain. It is not, however, fuel for real connection. It's fuel that runs hot, burns fast, and leaves a trail of polluted emotion. And if we live with any level of self-awareness, it's also the kind of intimacy that can leave us with the intense regrets of an integrity hangover. *Did I really participate in that? Is that moving us forward? Am I engaging in, quite literally, the exact same behavior that I find loathsome in others?*[2]

I understand how common enemy intimacy works in spiritual communities, because I participated in it through cynicism against anything that felt remotely similar to fundamentalism. But common enemy intimacy did not help me heal from fundamentalism, because it was the same judgment and spiritual superiority I hated in fundamentalism, but now with incense! We understandably end up forming these types of relationships because we have been hurt, but in response to hurt we need to be able to heal, and this won't heal us. Considering how common enemy intimacy and alcohol try to discharge pain without healing it, is it any surprise that the mixture of the two—especially in spiritual communities

2. Brené Brown, *Braving the Wilderness: The Quest for True Belonging and the Courage to Stand Alone* (New York: Random House, 2017), 136. Emphasis original.

built on sacred texts of healing—results in communities that will need to heal themselves before they can offer healing to anyone else?

The impact of connecting alcohol to identity is grave on the personal and communal levels because this connection is integrally related to our minds, bodies, and souls. The ways we are formed by identity can be conscious and subconscious, and our identity shapes everything—from what we say to how we pray, all the way down to our daily habits.

The habit part is especially important, because habits become some of the biggest barriers we face if we decide to change our relationship with alcohol. James Clear, in *Atomic Habits*, explains how we often try to change habits on the basis of our hopes for what we want to achieve, but he suggests identity-based habits, which focus on who we wish to become.[3] This is powerful, he writes, because "when your behavior and your identity are aligned, you are no longer pursuing behavior change. You are simply acting like the type of person you already believe you are," and moving toward a positive relationship between who we are and how we act is motivational.[4] However, there's always a flip side, and this one is vital if we want to change our relationship with alcohol: "The biggest barrier to positive change at any level— individual, team, society—is identity conflict."[5] So then, becoming mindful about our relationship with alcohol would allow us, at any level—individual, team, society—to move out of the identity conflict keeping us stuck in destructive habits.

3. James Clear, *Atomic Habits: An Easy and Proven Way to Build Good Habits and Break Bad Ones* (New York: Avery, 2018), 31.
4. Clear, *Atomic Habits*, 34–35.
5. Clear, *Atomic Habits*, 35.

Additionally, mindlessness regarding a culture of drug use in our community often means we don't take responsibility for the destructive jokes and general messaging about alcohol. When we do this, we help to fuel the identity crisis that keeps people stuck in harm. It is our responsibility to change those practices in our community.

Spirituality is a bid for connection with Spirit and self, but using alcohol as a bid for connection in our communities results in exclusivity because it alienates people who are wary of using drugs to form relationships. This bid for connection also ultimately leads to disconnection as alcohol can cause anxiety or depression or lead to strains on relationships because of what people do or say while intoxicated. The common refrain of "all are welcome" must ring true when a person changes their relationship with alcohol, so much so that those who have awakened to God and themselves through sobriety and mindfulness want to tell their spiritual community about the beautiful change in their lives. Unfortunately, perpetuating alcohol culture in spiritual spaces means all aren't welcome, because the space either doesn't invite those stories or, through messaging, actively dismisses their beauty.

Surviving Deconstruction

In the earliest days of my sober curiosity, much as during my movement out of fundamentalism, I kept my mouth shut. My deconstruction from drinking culture was no less raw and grievous than the deconstruction before it. I still cling to the words of the Book of Common Prayer, but now my questions are about why my sobriety makes me feel alien to the Church, why my anger is at the very spiritual home that offered me safe haven, and why I'm leaning so far into the mystery of God that I'm willing to give up my health insurance in order to fight against our culture's overwhelming encouragement of addiction.

Yet I won't stop believing in a liberating God, and if I can survive deconstructing fundamentalism and alcohol culture, I can survive anything. I had to lose fundamentalism to find God; I had to lose alcohol to find myself. In finding God and myself, something new awakened in me spiritually; my life changed and I was overcome with the presence of the Spirit resting upon me, which I received with a clarity I knew only sobriety could provide.

Deconstruction asked me to examine what I had always been told about God and to challenge it, question it, and notice how I might have been told things that were untrue. I began to wonder whether the voices I had trusted were worthy of my trust. It was grievous, because there was loss, as well as grief's best friend: anger. And yet deconstructing my faith led me into a relationship with God, myself, and the world around me that was joyful, rooted in trust, connected to truth, and abundant. My awakening in sobriety took on the same form as I went through the heartbreaking process of seeing how I had been taught lies about alcohol, such as that it has health benefits. I had to own my role in perpetuating the harm of alcohol. I had to wake up to how alcohol (its use and the criminalization of its use) is weaponized against marginalized communities and their ability to thrive, and I had to recognize how alcohol fuels internal messages of self-hatred and shame.

While the notion of deconstructing our understandings of sobriety might feel daunting, mindfulness around alcohol invites us into the possibility of a joyful relationship with God, ourselves, and the world. When I think of the barriers before us, I'm immediately reminded of a huge part of this work that I'll keep talking about: cognitive dissonance. To put it simply, cognitive dissonance is the experience of tension between our beliefs and our actions. Because we are built to avoid discomfort, we find reasons to reject whatever information suggests we are acting outside our beliefs so that we can justify our actions. This lowers our discomfort because we've found a way to match our beliefs and actions. Different insights we hear might show us a loophole so we can try to escape the dissonance by avoiding information that would help us reckon with the disconnect between our beliefs and actions. The more I learn about alcohol, the more I realize how much time and energy our culture has spent creating structures to offer us loopholes out of our cognitive dissonance around alcohol. We construct loopholes in regard to both drinking and sobriety, which creates a double whammy.

Here's how the double whammy might unfold. Pay attention the next time a public figure with a problematic relationship with drugs or a celebrity who is in recovery gets canceled or criticized for their actions. Often the comments aren't just about whatever caught the eye of the news: people will add that the person is a drunk or an addict, making the sweeping generalization that the person never should have been trusted in the first place because of their struggle with drugs. The comments will likely make a false connection between people who struggle with substances and people who cause harm. By all means, hold people accountable for their wrong actions, but if we can't do this without making connections that stigmatize people who struggle, we perpetuate the harm we criticize. Even if a celebrity hasn't done something wrong, being publicly sober can bring harsh criticism. I've witnessed how, after sober comedians do something silly in a TikTok video, people in the comments start suggesting that they have probably relapsed—as if it's impossible to be entertaining without being high. These commenters might think they're just commenting on the news, but they're revealing judgment and lack of compassion for people who struggle by associating such people with harm and dishonesty. Don't forget that your friends see your comments. Message received by the sober curious: I will be judged for struggling with alcohol, whether I get sober or not, and people won't be able to trust me.

Now, couple these types of sweeping judgments with the cultural message that quitting drinking makes you boring, or that it excludes you from social connections, because we need alcohol to experience fun and community. When people tweet "a dry party isn't a party!" or complain about how boring it was to go to a dry wedding (as if a couple's job on one of the most beautiful and intimate days of their lives is to pay for us to get a buzz), their friends who are secretly sober are also on Twitter. And we can read the comments, plus the replies. Or how about the fact that churches, in an attempt to "bring in more people," offer events that are often centered on drinking—as if alcohol is the draw, a way we show possible newcomers we are "fun"? Message received by the sober curious: the people I love perceive sober people as not fun and alcohol as central to building community, and if I quit, I will lose people and communities I care about.

With these scenarios in place, the fears of judgment, losing friends, and losing community work together to keep people drinking past the point when they might want to stop or change how they drink, and these fears keep them so overwhelmed that they don't know how to ask for help. It often goes like this:

- I don't like how I drink. I have this nagging feeling that my drinking isn't good for me.
- But sobriety doesn't seem fun, exciting, or aligned with who I am or how I wish to live my life.
- I'm stuck in the dissonance. I don't like how I drink, but quitting would appear to attack my identity, given what I've been told about drinking and sobriety.
- To escape the dissonance, I'm trying to reconcile my drinking with the gut feeling that these patterns are making my life more miserable, because I'm afraid I'll lose my friends. So, even in the face of mounting evidence that I don't like how I drink and want things to change, I'm also subconsciously trying to find ways to preserve my current way of life.
- Even when someone who has quit describes their drinking in a way that captures my own drinking habits, my inner voice will counter: if you had a problem, x, y, or z would have happened already.
- In the swirl of the conflict, seeking a way out of the challenge, cognitive dissonance has one very specific message for me: x, y, and z haven't happened, so you don't have a problem—and you can't be expected to live without friends.

Cognitive dissonance rarely happens because of one specific instance. This is why the messaging—both direct and indirect—is hugely significant. What might feel like silly tweets or comments among friends are all ways in which we could be alienating people who are struggling, encouraging our friends to stay in patterns of self-harm, and showing our true beliefs to our favorite people in the world without ever realizing it. This accidental alienation, encouragement toward self-harm, and revelation of hurtful beliefs affect the souls of the both the messenger and the recipient.

The messaging I received about hurtful theology worked in much the same way. Sometimes it was direct, at other times implied. Over time, messages are received, and those messages shape how we show up in the world, whether we feel loved, whether we feel connected to God, and whether we take the chance of revealing to the outside world who we truly are inside our souls. The great news amid the challenges of messaging is that, as we have learned through so many people who are now healing from the trauma of Christian fundamentalism, healing is available. Healing from fundamentalism requires truthbearers: people willing to receive the hard truth and change their ways, acting with the courage to challenge the status quo. Healing from the harm caused by promotion of alcohol will require the same kind of truthbearers. Changing oppressive dominant messaging can bring the toxicity that threatens us out into the open, and only when we reveal the wound can healing begin.

If we let it, changing our relationship with alcohol can mean entering the joy that is equal parts terror and amazement, and inside that joy we can, as beloved children of God, be freed from some of our harm and awakened to a way of life that lets us show up in the world more fully. Through the clarity this work provides and our decision to be sober or drink differently, we can better trust that we are loved and connected to God without the barriers of alcohol-induced shame. We can also be freed from our judgment about others, which surely brightens and lightens the soul.

I often imagine what our world, and our spiritual communities, might look like if we took a chance on revealing to the outside world who we truly are. I believe with all my soul that our world, and our spiritual lives, will thrive if we face how messages around alcohol have caused harm. But this must be done in a way that doesn't foster shame, because shame will only send us back into harm. I believe we will thrive if we turn toward healing our relationship with alcohol, such that we can release the alcohol-laden messages calling us to numb ourselves. Only then will we create a heart of spirituality that understands itself as a primary way to reduce the harm of alcohol. A sober spirituality will allow us to usher people into the fullness of who they are, release the judgment that takes us away from God and ourselves, love others deeply amid any condition of humanity, nourish the spiritual closeness that can offer peace, and bear witness to the beauty of a world full of people who are trying to be awakened to themselves, one another, and the Spirit.

refresh and reflect

Think about some of the messages you have received over time.

- Alcohol: What do you believe alcohol offers you?
- Spiritual community: What makes being in a spiritual community meaningful?
- Identity: What parts of yourself feel most important to you?

how alcohol affects the body

Countering Common Myths about Alcohol's Benefits

WHETHER IT'S RITUAL WASHING, anointing with oil, or prayer over meals, spirituality has always been connected to the body. In Hebrew Scripture, we learn how God is so mindful of our bodies, ravens have been known to come to us bearing food when we are on the brink of death.

Caring for our bodies is not just about self-preservation; it is also about worship. We are encouraged to care for our bodies because we are encouraged to love, tend, and be stewards of creation, and our own bodies are a part of creation. When we care for our bodies in tangible ways, these are outward and visible signs of inward and spiritual grace. As we hear more about creation care and its necessity, we might also extend this care to ourselves.

Care for the body in response to alcohol is not a fix-all; it is a way for us to start noticing the way drinking affects our bodies so that we can begin to change how we care for ourselves. It is wisdom that can help us mitigate harm.

In order to provide this care for our bodies, we first have to reckon with some facts and statistics regarding alcohol's effects. Full disclosure: we're going to get into some of the findings and statistics around patterns and habits with alcohol to help us understand the pervasive and damaging nature of alcohol culture. I share this not to shame you, dear reader, but to help you overcome any notion that you are alone. I also cannot, with any integrity, invite you into a deeper connection with your mind, body, and soul without acknowledging how your mind, body, and soul are affected by this drug. Recall the words of Frederick Buechner, "The gospel is bad news before it is good news."[1] I remember reading through many of these statistics in my earliest sober curiosity and being overwhelmed by the feeling that it was bad news, that I was bad news. I couldn't have known then that it was, in fact, good news because it invited me into a different way of treating my mind, body, and soul.

When I was trying to sustain sobriety, I joined an online sobriety community named Tempest, which offered a module titled "Alcohol and the Brain." I never expected studying neuroscience to be liberating, but it was. I don't connect with the moral failure model of addiction, which teaches that a challenging relationship with alcohol is due to a person's poor choices and moral failings; yet, I don't strictly follow the disease model either, which suggests that one can trace

1. Frederick Buechner, *Telling the Truth: The Gospel as Tragedy, Comedy, and Fairy Tale* (New York: HarperCollins, 1977), 7.

the origin of a challenging relationship with alcohol to a person's biology, neurology, and genetics. Instead, to understand a challenging relationship with alcohol, I look at the whole of human life. This includes our genetics, our social context, the ways we have received support from childhood to now, how support has been unavailable to us over time, the beliefs that have shaped how we understand our worth, trauma and the way it acts on the soul, whether we are encouraged toward rest and joy, how we have been oppressed because of who we were created to be by God, the realities of how ethanol acts on a human brain, and more. For me, learning that my challenging relationship with alcohol was linked to my brain and the natural functions of my body—alongside trauma and other chapters of my life from childhood to now—removed just enough shame that I could go all in on changing my relationship with alcohol.

Reckoning with Cognitive Dissonance

Let's start our examination of the facts about drinking with some common beliefs about alcohol that can serve as ways out of our dissonance:

Alcohol helps us sleep.
Alcohol helps us unwind.
Alcohol is legal.
Alcohol has health benefits.

If a person begins to question their drinking but feels fearful about how quitting would be difficult, the above statements can serve as a way for them to escape their cognitive dissonance. Here's another example of how this might work:

- I've been looking at ways to improve my health, and it doesn't seem to make sense that I would avoid chemicals in my food but then put ethanol in my body.

- But I'm an extrovert and community has always been really important to me. I get anxious in social situations and drinking helps me loosen up.

- I'm stuck in the dissonance. I'm worried that drinking may be unhealthy for me, but I fear that if I quit drinking, I won't be able to make connections and be social anymore.

- To try to escape the dissonance, I'm hoping to find a way to reconcile my drinking with my health, because the risk of losing connection is seemingly impossible, but I care about what I put in my body. Even in the face of the mounting evidence that alcohol is bad for my health, I'm trying to find ways to preserve my current way of life.

- I'm reading health articles about alcohol, and many say it is harmful, but I remember also hearing that it is good for my heart.

- Even when I read about the harm of a relationship with alcohol that seems similar to my drinking habits, my inner voice keeps saying that if I had a problem my doctor would have flagged it.

- In the swirl of the conflict, seeking a way out of the challenge, cognitive dissonance has one very specific message for me: red wine is good for your heart.

To resolve cognitive dissonance, we have to either change our beliefs or change our actions. Before I was ready to stop drinking, I kept changing the belief over and over, looking for a way to frame it differently. I could prop up "alcohol helps me sleep" for a little while, until I found myself Googling sleep doctors. I could prop up "alcohol helps me unwind," until I found myself back at the doctor's office sharing how my anxiety hadn't improved. Meanwhile, I was doing things I wasn't proud of when I drank, and I didn't have anything to prop that up, so I went straight down the shame hole. Each time I propped something up I watched it fall down, until finally I knew my actions had to change.

Everyone will have to reckon with both their actions and their beliefs—in alcohol and in everything else—in order to reconcile themselves to their professed values. I had to research my way into recognizing that none of the one-liners I heard could support my drinking. Discernment requires reckoning with the one-liners regardless of where we end up, so let's reckon with four of the most prominent ones.

Alcohol Helps Us Sleep

Alcohol consumption, whether mild or severe, not only impedes sleep but can also induce sleep disorders. The way alcohol impacts sleep adds to the risk of major illnesses connected to lack of sleep, such as depressive disorders, heart disease, and others. Because alcohol already increases the risk of these diseases, the link between alcohol's disruption of sleep and our health raises grave concerns.[2] Statistics aside, ask

2. Soon-Yeob Park et al., "The Effects of Alcohol on Quality of Sleep," *Korean Journal of Family Medicine* 36, no. 6 (2015): 294–99, https://doi.org/10.4082/kjfm.2015.36.6.294.

yourself this: Does drinking help you sleep, or does it merely help you get to sleep? As a recovery coach, I hear from many of my clients that alcohol helps them get to sleep, but the quality of sleep is poor, and sometimes even reduced drinking results in improved quality of sleep. Sleep is rest, Sabbath, and it gives us the capacity we need to foster and receive joy, and we don't receive good sleep by consuming alcohol.

Alcohol Helps Us Unwind

While the immediate effects of alcohol serve to depress your central nervous system and make you feel more relaxed, large quantities of alcohol and usage of it over time spike anxiety. Additionally, your body will begin to build a tolerance to the immediate way alcohol acts to mellow you out, which can make anxiety and stress harder to cope with.[3] Physiological effects aside, alcohol can impair judgment, leading to decisions that cause shame and major consequences, which cause anxiety to skyrocket. Medical studies show that anxiety is actually a comorbidity with alcohol use disorder, because instead of helping us unwind, alcohol fuels the feeling that we're trying to escape. The anxiety caused by alcohol withholds our joy from us.

Alcohol Is Legal

A cursory look at the history of drugs and legality suggests that the war on drugs was purposely created to instill racist and classist policies—not out of a desire to help people but to further marginalize and oppress ethnically diverse populations while preserving White upper-class drug use. "Drugs

3. Kristeen Cherney, "Alcohol and Anxiety," Healthline, September 26, 2019, https://www.healthline.com/health/alcohol-and-anxiety#alcohol-effects.

and alcohol" messaging was designed to go after "drug users" while creating the image of a "drug user" as a non-White person.[4] To this day, the language of "drugs and alcohol" allows our society to see people who drink as different from people who "use drugs," even though drinking is drug use. In terms of legality, being in a position of privilege means ending up with legal troubles due to a challenging relationship with drugs but being able to get out of those troubles, while non-White or low-income people in similar circumstances are more likely to end up in prison.

Even if we avoid the racism and classism around alcohol and legality, legality doesn't prove that something is good. Statistically, as of 2020, one person dies every forty-five minutes because of a drunk driving crash in the United States. A blood alcohol concentration (BAC) of 0.08 percent or higher is considered legal grounds for a DUI citation, but a legal limit doesn't define alcohol's safety or repercussions. This is proved by the fact that in 2020, 2,041 people died in drunk driving crashes where the driver had a blood alcohol content of 0.01 to 0.07 percent.[5] So the amount a person drinks might be legal but still result in preventable deaths.

Alcohol is a drug that can lead to disastrous consequences, including 3.3 million fatalities globally each year.[6] Alcohol's legality upholds its widespread acceptance, which makes it one of the most serious addictions modern society faces. In

4. Maia Szalavitz, *Undoing Drugs: The Untold Story of Harm Reduction and the Future of Addiction* (New York: Hachette, 2021), 117.
5. "Drunk Driving," National Highway Traffic Safety Administration, November 12, 2021, https://www.nhtsa.gov/risky-driving/drunk-driving.
6. "Alcohol," World Health Organization, May 9, 2022, https://www.who.int /news-room/fact-sheets/detail/alcohol#:~:text=Key%20facts,represents%20 5.3%25%20of%20all%20deaths.

the same spirit as drug policy makers who sought to serve not public health but control over the disenfranchised, the promotion of mindless alcohol use keeps people of privilege in power by making their drug use a status symbol, regardless of consequences, and promotes the narrative that non-White and poor people should be jailed. When we perpetuate this, we act against joy for all people and ourselves.

Alcohol Has Health Benefits

Picture it—I know you can: someone at a party lifts their glass, the cabernet almost spilling from the top, cheering, "For my heart!" I know I have made the joke myself, taking another full glass of red wine from the bladder of the box. It's a common sentiment, immortalized on kitchen towels and in memes, but through it we let out a laugh of release, not knowing—or ignoring—that the health we toast is the butt of the joke.

In 2019 the American Heart Association (AHA) published an article titled "Drinking Red Wine for Heart Health? Read This before You Toast," which reveals that no research has established a cause-and-effect link between drinking alcohol and better heart health.[7] It's been said that red wine is good for the heart because it has antioxidants, specifically resveratrol, which can be found in the skin of grapes, in peanuts, and in blueberries. However, the idea that resveratrol is healthy for the heart is contested. Additionally, if it is good for the heart, to get enough resveratrol for it to be helpful you'd have

---

7. "Drinking Red Wine for Heart Health? Read This before You Toast," *American Heart Association News*, May 24, 2019, https://www.heart.org/en/news/2019/05/24/drinking-red-wine-for-heart-health-read-this-before-you-toast.

to drink to excess, and drinking to excess is known to increase the risk of illness, not protect the heart. The AHA suggests that if a person decides to drink, they should drink moderately (no more than one to two drinks per day for people assigned male at birth and one drink per day for people assigned female at birth, with one drink equaling 12 ounces of beer, 4 ounces of wine, 1.5 ounces of 80-proof spirits, or 1 ounce of 100-proof spirits).

Drinking to excess has dire effects on the heart: it can cause high blood pressure, promote arrhythmias, and put us at higher risk of cardiomyopathy, which makes alcohol toxic to the heart and can result in heart failure.[8] Aside from heart health, alcohol is connected to liver damage, many types of cancer, and other diseases. It would seem that if we claim health as a reason to drink, the science shows we are better off adding grapes, peanuts, and blueberries to our diet to get that resveratrol.

The AHA gives us a definition of drinking moderately, but how often do we drink moderately? One standard bottle of wine—750 milliliters—contains 6.35 servings of wine. I share this because when I was drinking most, I was sometimes drinking a bottle of wine in one night. Most often I was drinking from boxes of wine that were harder to measure. I filled my wine glass to what looked like full to me (not even to the very tip top), and I would have told you I had consumed x glasses of wine in a night, but I was really drinking significantly more. If you couple the common mismeasurement of our drinking with the fact that between 40 percent and 60 percent of alcohol use is not reported, we learn how the

---

8. "Drinking Red Wine for Heart Health?"

already grave alcohol statistics don't fully capture the extent of our culture's alcohol crisis.[9]

Reclaiming Joy

If we are going to talk about the spiritual effects of alcohol, we have to acknowledge the way alcohol can impact our day-to-day joy. Changing my relationship with alcohol had major positive effects on my anxiety and depression, but I didn't put it together until I had quit for about two months. The reduction in anxiety and depression caused by sobriety allowed me to connect with my soul more deeply. I assumed I would feel better if I didn't drink, but I thought it would be because I wasn't ashamed of my actions; I couldn't have anticipated the lift in my mood caused just by removing alcohol from my body or how my body came into balance, spiritually and mentally, because I wasn't guzzling a depressant.

Alcohol and anxiety, and alcohol and depression, are common comorbidities. Struggling with anxiety and depression can send us toward unhealthy drinking patterns as we try to cope, but coping with alcohol only creates more reasons why we need to cope. Studies reveal that the act of drinking in and of itself can send us into states of anxiety and depression even for those who have not previously struggled with anxiety and depression. Anxiety and alcohol use disorder are so intricately woven together that it's hard to tell whether people with anxiety disorders are more likely to become dependent

9. Sadie Boniface, James Kneale, and Nicola Shelton, "Drinking Pattern Is More Strongly Associated with Under-Reporting of Alcohol Consumption Than Socio-Demographic Factors: Evidence from a Mixed-Methods Study," *PubMed Central*, December 18, 2014, https://www.ncbi.nlm.nih.gov/pmc/articles/PMC43 20509/.

on alcohol because they use it to self-medicate or whether people who struggle with anxiety do so largely because of the repercussions of inevitable alcohol withdrawal.[10]

Drinking can decrease the likelihood of recovery from anxiety disorders, because alcohol increases anxiety, creating a feedback loop leading to exacerbation of both the dependence on alcohol and the anxiety. Anxiety disorders are likely to increase the severity, persistence, and poor treatment response of alcohol use disorder, and alcohol use disorder returns the favor by increasing the severity, persistence, and poor treatment response of anxiety disorders. The same patterns are often present between alcohol and depression, and a person struggling with depression might use alcohol to cope, even though the alcohol contributes to the need for coping, creating yet another feedback loop.[11]

When I was drinking, I had good days and bad days just like anyone else. I did not realize how alcohol was affecting my mental health until I quit. Many years ago, I took an antidepressant for the first time. Later that night I found myself at a bar, declining a drink. I explained (because we have to explain declining a drink) that I was on antidepressants. The bartender laughed, saying, "Everyone drinks on antidepressants." I had that one night of no drinking on antidepressants, then it was back to my norm. And the man wasn't wrong—lots of people drink on antidepressants—but when I got sober, I realized how hard alcohol worked against my antidepressant,

10. Joshua P. Smith and Carrie L. Randall, "Anxiety and Alcohol Use Disorders," *Alcohol Research: Current Reviews* 34, no. 4 (2012): 414–31, https://www.ncbi .nlm.nih.gov/pmc/articles/PMC3860396/.

11. Mary W. Kuria et al., "The Association between Alcohol Dependence and Depression before and after Treatment for Alcohol Dependence," *ISRN Psychiatry*, 2012, https://www.ncbi.nlm.nih.gov/pmc/articles/PMC3658562/.

because alcohol is a depressant. Alcohol is a drug that works against the natural chemicals in your body trying to source joy for you, which means it also works against the prescription chemicals in your body trying to keep you afloat. Sobriety means I don't drink a depressant daily, and my mental health reflects the choice. What I used to consider "good days" are at a level I would now call a "bad day," and what I now consider to be my day-to-day norm was previously understood to be something akin to a mythical Best Day of My Life.

Drinking a depressant as a norm kept my baseline of joy incredibly low; sobriety lifted my baseline, such that I am consistently in a happier place. I still take meds and meet with a therapist—I even added in a psychiatrist for good measure—but my sober bad days are what I used to consider the general experience of just being alive, and my sober good days are beyond what I imagined for myself, because sobriety made my day-to-day life more positive. Entering into joy and reducing harm means noticing how alcohol might be exacerbating some of your challenges—it means becoming mindful about how you drink and the state of your mind, body, and soul.

What about Withdrawal?

We can't talk about the harmful effects of alcohol without acknowledging the harmful effects of quitting alcohol. Alcohol depresses the body's systems, which eventually slows down the brain and makes it harder for your nerves to talk to each other. Your central nervous system then has to work to keep your brain as alert as possible while trying to help your struggling nervous system, all just to manage the alcohol in your body.[12] When you end a drinking episode, your brain stays in this alert state, which causes withdrawal. Withdrawal causes a range of symptoms, some arriving only six hours after you quit, but others showing up forty-eight to seventy-two hours later. Symptoms include anxiety, headache, nausea, insomnia, and body sweats, among other ailments. Withdrawal in its most severe stage (sometimes called delirium tremens, occurring forty-eight to seventy-two hours after the end of the drinking episode) can include delusions, hallucinations, and even seizures.

Care for alcohol withdrawal can include everything from getting some support and nourishment for the body to hospitalization. The kind of care needed is best assessed by a medical professional. That said, many who struggle don't have access to a medical professional. If you are in that situation, I encourage you to check whether there is a harm reduction community in your area with access to free resources and to explore HAMS: Harm Reduction for Alcohol. HAMS, which stands for Harm reduction, Abstinence, and Moderation Support, is a free peer-led space where you can find support and learn more about changing drinking habits.[13]

Withdrawal is never a sign of moral failure. Rather, it's a physical reaction, and we should try to change our hearts so we don't see it as a failure. Remember: hangovers and alcohol withdrawal present with very similar symptoms. Both signal that the body is trying to come back to homeostasis after a drinking episode. In fact, plenty of people might be facing

12. Mary Jo DiLonardo, "What Is Alcohol Withdrawal?," WebMD, November 26, 2021, https://www.webmd.com/mental-health/addiction/alcohol-withdrawal-symptoms-treatments#1.
13. HAMS: Harm Reduction for Alcohol, https://hams.cc/.

withdrawal every morning but calling it a hangover because they don't quit long enough to know whether it is a sign of a deeper dependence. We can choose to let an experience of a hangover be a way in which we empathetically connect to those going through withdrawal. If a person is trying not to drink and then becomes aware of their body's dependence on alcohol, their mindfulness deserves support.

Withdrawal, like any other side effect, deserves care, compassion, and support, yet people suffering through withdrawal often don't receive this love. While I reserve my anger for systems, not individuals, our society often demonizes the person suffering in addiction before it questions the motives of a $250 billion alcohol industry. Jesus reminds us that we can't serve two masters because we will hate one and love the other or be devoted to one and despise the other, which supports the conclusion no one seems to want to take literally: "You cannot serve both God and money" (Matt. 6:24 NIV). When we judge those who are suffering from withdrawal but fail to look for accountability from the alcohol industry, we are choosing our master.

Spiritual communities could become places where people feel safe to go when they struggle with drugs, not communities they fear might find out. Spiritual communities could save lives through providing various forms of care: harm reduction peer support, people to monitor physical symptoms, food to nourish people's bodies, connections to support and care for those who choose to go through a tapering process—all of which would help reduce harm, illness, death, and more. Sometimes when a person is struggling with withdrawal, it's because they are actively trying to quit, and that is cause for celebration. We should be greeting them in the beautiful act of trying to heal with ways to help keep them on the path to joy. Belief in hope and resurrection means being in opposition to anyone dying because they are trying to heal.

Finding Hope in a Healing God

These truths are offered with hope—awareness is the first step. While cognitive dissonance can hold us in behaviors that don't serve us, it can also help us see the disconnect between our actions and our beliefs, which can invite us to use different actions to resolve the conflict and to offer ourselves greater care. I'm a harm reductionist at heart, so my hope is not to convince everyone to quit drinking but to invite everyone into the process of discerning how we are in relationship with alcohol, because alcohol is affecting our minds, bodies, souls, and health. But we do not live as those without hope, because there is hope not just in abstinence from alcohol but in harm reduction. Nothing is impossible with God; steps can be taken to bring more gentleness and care into your mind, body, and soul—just through changing your relationship with alcohol.

One of the things I love about the healing ministry of Jesus is that no condition of human life is outside his care. Nothing can exclude us from worthiness, whether it be our choice to drink or something else we face. Drinking has tremendous stigma around it, in part because society places so much of the blame on the individual. But in the midst of a swirl of studies, hear this: your relationship with alcohol is not in a vacuum. There's a reason you've been taught what you've been taught, there are reasons you have needed to cope, there are core messages telling you alcohol is a necessary part of a flourishing human life, and this is not your fault. If we are burdened by the truth of how alcohol hurts these bodies entrusted to our care and the people we love, we can make individual choices and also uphold each other in love. We can end the messaging that perpetuates this harm, doing so in order to reach healing, while knowing we do this best when we do it for ourselves and for others.

God's healing power is at work when Antabuse is used to deter drinking in the same way that God's healing power is at work when Narcan restores life to those who overdose on drugs. Similarly, God's healing power is in the coffee and conversation of the faithful twelve-steppers. God loves you whether you drink or you get sober. Healing is noncompetitive and, in order for us to heal and be ushered into joy, it must meet us where we are right now, where the Spirit always waits for us.

refresh and reflect

Recognizing the truth of how alcohol affects the body is a difficult process, so it's important to remember that this truth is intended to lead you toward a deeper care for your body. Today, practice caring for your body, whether by taking a nap, feeding yourself something delicious, moving your body in a way you enjoy, or engaging in another body-care practice you love.

freedom from deception

Exposing the Lies of the Alcohol Industry

IT MAY NOT SURPRISE YOU that a girl who got saved at a hell house has heard a little bit about deception, usually personified as the one and only: Satan. Hebrew Scripture depicts Satan as a serpent, a character defined by being conniving and manipulative. Religious or not, people know about the serpent and Satan. The Greek word transliterated *diabolos*, which is often translated as *devil*, depicts an accuser, a slanderer, a purveyor of lies and deception. And most of Christianity professes to be in direct opposition to the powers and principalities that destroy the creatures of God—those powers and principalities that take on Satan's character and behavior, which is to slander, deceive, and lead us away from truth.

Care for the soul and going inward are primary to the calling of bringing mindfulness into our relationship with alcohol, but this spiritual care can't just be self-serving and internal. We must also pursue truth, because truth is a bedrock of the mindfulness required, as well as the bedrock out of which we learn what truly nourishes the soul. Deception is the enemy of joy, and deception is fueling our lack of access to knowledge about alcohol and the harm done to us in mind, body, and soul by drinking mindlessly.

In 2014, Laura A. Stokowski wrote an article titled "No Amount of Alcohol Is Safe," and in August 2018, Robyn Burton and Nick Sheron published the article "No Level of Alcohol Consumption Improves Health," but I don't imagine these articles were brought up at your cocktail parties or shared on Facebook as often as the articles about the "health benefits" of booze.[1] As a culture, we avoid talking about how the ethanol in your cocktail is also the ethanol in your gasoline. The beverages we serve at parties aren't too far away from the gasoline that, if it got on your hands, would prompt you to quickly wash up. If it shouldn't sit too long on your hands, why should it be processed by your body? The truth about the dangers of alcohol will continue to be drowned out by the projected $7.7 billion to be spent on alcohol advertising alone in 2023.[2] The pervasive nature of alcohol advertising doesn't surprise me: when I tweet about my sobriety, or tweet any

---

1. Laura A. Stokowski, "No Amount of Alcohol Is Safe," Medscape, April 30, 2014, https://www.medscape.com/viewarticle/824237_0; Robyn Burton and Nick Sheron, "No Level of Alcohol Consumption Improves Health," *The Lancet* 392, no. 10152 (2018): 987–88, https://doi.org/10.1016/S0140-6736(18)31571-X.

2. "Business Intelligence—Alcohol: Beer + Spirits," Zenith: The ROI Agency, October 15, 2021, https://movendi.ngo/wp-content/uploads/2021/05/Business-Intelligence-Alcohol-Beer-and-Spirits.pdf.

criticism of alcohol, I always immediately see a sponsored booze tweet on my feed, because the advertising algorithm knows what it's doing, and it certainly doesn't exist to respect my sobriety.

In September 2018, the World Health Organization released its global status report on alcohol and health, specifically naming alcohol culture for what it is: a global health crisis.[3] Unfortunately, I don't remember people in 2018 being overly concerned about the report and what it entailed. I don't remember people radically changing our society's way of life to try to alter the fact that, like COVID-19, alcohol kills—especially since alcohol has been killing people for much longer, with a count of three million alcohol-related deaths per year starting as far back as 2016.[4] In the wake of COVID-19, churches, schools, grocery stores, and friendships changed in response to a threat of death. However, when alcohol was and is named as having the same death toll, very little changes. Now we even know that in 2020 more adults under the age of sixty-five died from alcohol-related complications than from COVID-19.[5] Our culture's overwhelming challenge with alcohol is worthy of the same level of global acknowledgment and societal change in order to mitigate its deadly effects.

But it's not just that we are ignorant about the harms of alcohol. The deception goes deeper. In March 2018, the *New*

3. "Global Status Report on Alcohol and Health 2018," World Health Organization, September 27, 2018, https://www.who.int/publications/i/item/9789241 565639.

4. "Alcohol Use in the United States," National Institute on Alcohol Abuse and Alcoholism, March 2022, https://www.niaaa.nih.gov/publications/brochures -and-fact-sheets/alcohol-facts-and-statistics.

5. Roni Caryn Rabin, "Alcohol-Related Deaths Spiked during the Pandemic, a Study Shows," *New York Times*, March 22, 2022, https://www.nytimes.com/2022 /03/22/health/alcohol-deaths-covid.html.

York Times published the article "Federal Agency Courted Alcohol Industry to Fund Study on Benefits of Moderate Drinking."[6] Senior federal health officials created a campaign for a clinical study with the hopes of finally delivering all the medical evidence necessary to recommend alcohol as part of a healthy American diet, requesting financial support from the audiences where they spoke. Who was the audience for these presentations, you ask? Alcohol industry executives. The study, which has since been shut down, was to be overseen by the National Institute on Alcohol Abuse and Alcoholism (NIAAA), one of twenty-seven centers under the National Institutes of Health (NIH). Leadership within both the NIAAA and the NIH falsely reported that there was no connection between the study and the alcohol industry.

These federal agencies paid for scientists to travel and meet with alcohol industry executives to pitch the study by arguing that it would help promote alcohol use and hence would be worth funding. Health officials promised that the executives could preview the way the study would be done and could have the opportunity to vet investigators in the study. After industry executives had seen the presentation, health officials followed up with further appeals for money. Health officials went so far as to claim that "by design, no form of alcohol—wine, liquor or beer—would be called out as better than another in the trial."[7] The *New York Times* article even reveals that the NIH has a policy prohibiting "employees

6. Roni Caryn Rabin, "Federal Agency Courted Alcohol Industry to Fund Study on Benefits of Moderate Drinking," *New York Times*, March 17, 2018, https://www.nytimes.com/2018/03/17/health/nih-alcohol-study-liquor-industry.html.
7. Rabin, "Federal Agency Courted Alcohol Industry."

from soliciting or suggesting donations, funds or other resources intended to support activities"—a policy that would seem to have been violated by these actions.

One United Kingdom study on the connections between alcohol and cancer arose out of researchers' awareness of how the alcohol industry shares information about alcohol and cancer as a way of being socially responsible. Researchers looked through websites and documents from twenty-seven alcohol industry organizations. The study reveals that most of the organizations shared misrepresentations of the science about alcohol and cancer, using the following industry strategies: "(1) denial/omission: denying, omitting or disputing the evidence that alcohol consumption increases cancer risk; (2) distortion: mentioning cancer, but misrepresenting the risk; and (3) distraction: focusing discussion away from the independent effects of alcohol on common cancers. Breast cancer and colorectal cancer appeared to be a particular focus for this misrepresentation."[8] The final verdict? The alcohol industry is misrepresenting the truth about the harm alcohol can do to your body, especially regarding cancer. Researchers write, "This finding is important because the industry is involved in developing alcohol policy in many countries, and in disseminating health information to the public, including schoolchildren. Policymakers, academics, public health and other practitioners should reconsider the appropriateness of their relationships to these [alcohol industry] bodies."[9]

8. Mark Petticrew et al., "How Alcohol Industry Organisations Mislead the Public about Alcohol and Cancer," *Drug and Alcohol Review*, 37, no. 3 (2018): 293–303, https://doi.org/10.1111/dar.12596.

9. Petticrew et al., "How Alcohol Industry Organisations Mislead the Public."

Protections have been put in place to preserve the $250 billion alcohol industry, even at the expense of our joy.[10] It's an expense for our children too. David H. Jernigan led a study revealing that alcohol companies make $17.5 billion off underage drinking alone.[11] To make matters worse, in April 2018, *STAT* published an article titled "NIH Rejected a Study of Alcohol Advertising While Pursuing Industry Funding for Other Research," which revealed how, in 2015, NIH officials called together university scientists to present research that NIH had funded on the association between alcohol marketing and underage drinking. However, the officials became irate when the findings confirmed the harm alcohol marketing inflicts on youth.[12] This matters because we know there are three main factors that determine whether a person will struggle with alcohol use disorder (AUD): genetics and family history, trauma and mental health challenges, and underage drinking.

Want to know how I know those three factors? They are found on the website of the NIAAA, which states, "A recent national survey found that among people ages 26 and older, those who began drinking before age 15 were more than

10. Andrea Shalal and Diane Bartz, "Treasury Wants to Stir Up U.S. Alcohol Market to Help Smaller Players," *Reuters*, February 9, 2022, https://www.reuters.com/business/exclusive-treasury-wants-stir-up-us-alcohol-market-help-smaller-players-2022-02-09/.

11. David H. Jernigan, "Alcohol Companies Make $17.5 Billion a Year Off of Underage Drinking, While Prevention Efforts Are Starved for Cash," *The Conversation*, June 10, 2021, https://theconversation.com/alcohol-companies-make-17-5-billion-a-year-off-of-underage-drinking-while-prevention-efforts-are-starved-for-cash-162222.

12. Sharon Begley, "NIH Rejected a Study of Alcohol Advertising While Pursuing Industry Funding for Other Research," *STAT*, April 2, 2018, https://wwwapp.bumc.bu.edu/BEDAC_Camy/_docs/newsroom/in-the-news/PDFs-In%20the%20News/04%2002%2018%20NIH%20Rejected%20Study%20of%20Alcohol.pdf.

5 times as likely to report having AUD in the past year as those who waited until age 21 or later to begin drinking."[13] The money-making formula seems to be to ignore the harm caused by marketing alcohol to youth, because this increases the likelihood that they will suffer from addiction, which means sustained profits from long-term buyers.

A close friend and I have bonded through mocktail nights and our shared sense of humor. During one of these mocktail nights the subject of the best nonalcoholic beers came up, and I learned that my friend used to work in the beer industry. As I wrote this chapter, I reached out, shared the basic gist of my findings, and asked for their insight. I said to my friend what I'll say to you: I believe that systems deserve criticism and people deserve compassion. I knew I wanted to tell the truth about the alcohol industry while still showing compassion toward those who have worked in it.

The response they gave was telling. They explained how they had worked in alcohol sales and the toll the pressure took on them. They described the anxiety and depression, plus how these reactions were exacerbated by the cycles of numbing that were just part of the job. They told me about conferences in which their job had been to visit the bars selling the company's beer to pump the employees full of alcohol and incentivize the bars to sell more. They told me how they felt icky about what they were asked to do, describing it as "the most stressful time of my life." I share this to say that compassion toward the minds, bodies, and souls of all people means compassion toward people working in these

---

13. "Understanding Alcohol Use Disorder," National Institute on Alcohol Abuse and Alcoholism, April 2021, https://www.niaaa.nih.gov/publications /brochures-and-fact-sheets/understanding-alcohol-use-disorder.

industries. Systems deserve our criticism, while individuals deserve our compassion. My friend had agreed to work in this job for two years but left after one year. They couldn't stay any longer because of the drinking required and its negative impact on their mental health.

I hear passionate arguments all the time about the dangers of capitalism and how huge companies and industries cause harm, how they are corrupt, how they profit off injustice, and how working conditions are deplorable. The alcohol industry isn't just capitalism—it's one of the most insidious forms of capitalism imaginable. The alcohol industry directly profits off our minds, bodies, and souls by taking advantage of us, often when we are in pain. Those of us who rage against these billion-dollar industries could bring that "vote with your dollars" spirit to the consumption of alcohol. We all have to figure out how we will be consumers in a capitalistic world, making the best decisions given our circumstances. In the same way that we have begun to encourage mindful consumerism with the goal of joy for society as a whole, we must read the stories of workers in the alcohol industry—retaining our respect for them as individuals—and receive the truth of this industry's corruption and the death toll in its wake. We must let these factors influence what businesses we support.

Our culture is drinking an intentional and fatal cocktail, mixing equal parts deception from the alcohol industry, deception in health messaging, and deception upheld through advertising—all on the rocks of the human condition. If we care about being followers of the truth, we have to talk about how the alcohol industry has been serving up lies. The alcohol industry does not care how alcohol affects the quality of your life, and the public health officials who partner with the industry care more about their wealth than your health. At the end of the day, to the alcohol industry and the power aligned with it, it doesn't matter if you end up sick or if alcohol tucks you into your deathbed. It doesn't matter if your family stops speaking to you, if you have anxiety and depression, if you ever grow to love yourself—as long as they get your money. Your addiction is their profit, and it would hurt their business if you took them up on the half-hearted invitation to drink responsibly.

In order to grapple with healing mind, body, and soul, we will need more than medical journals and the words of officials. I trust the research I've shared, but I also recognize that it doesn't tell the whole story. Gathering information serves as a useful starting place, but I would encourage you to take that knowledge and discern your own way forward. It is in placing your finger on the pulse of your soul and life that the search for joy can best bear fruit.

refresh and reflect

In the wake of such challenging information, remember this: you can only know what you know. For many, this will be the first time you are hearing these truths about alcohol and how it affects society. Take a moment to acknowledge that you did not know this before, but you do know this now. Reflect on the following questions: What did you believe about alcohol before reading this? What do you believe about alcohol now?

the blood of Christ, the cup of salvation

Placing Alcohol within Scripture in Its Proper Context

WHILE I WAS IN SEMINARY, two professors transformed how I read Scripture. They introduced a framework for engaging the Bible: the world behind the text (the historical context of the specific passage), the world of the text (the cultural realities that would be influencing what was happening as well as the literary features of the passage), and the world in front of the text (the time between the event in Scripture and today).

The argument used to prop up cognitive dissonance around alcohol that upsets me the most is also the most common one in my world: Jesus drank wine! When we use this Scripture to perpetuate harmful understandings of booze, we betray the world behind the text, the world of the text, and the world in front of the text.

Alcohol within Scripture

Wine existed in Jesus's day, and we have every reason to believe he drank it. But there are major factors behind these truths that prohibit his imbibing from becoming a way we may uphold a toxic relationship between alcohol and spirituality. For one, consider the world behind the text: vintners in the ancient Near East didn't have the tools we have to avoid pests, so they often picked grapes earlier in the growth process, before the grapes became ripe and sweet enough to attract insects and birds. This earlier picking can result in lower alcohol levels in the wine due to less sugar in the grapes.[1] We don't know for sure whether wine at that time was wet farmed or dry farmed, though we do know the area struggled with dry seasons. Dry seasons could result in a richer wine with a higher alcohol count, so the mustum (unfermented pulp) from the grape was sometimes added as a way to stop fermentation before the wine became vinegar.[2] In light of this, it was common to dilute the wine. Anne Valdespino writes that this rich wine was "a plus for Roman centurions, hillside shepherds and Galilean fishermen who could carry a small amount in a skin and dilute it with water to create more servings."[3] It's possible that the dilution worked more like starting with a concentrate, not necessarily lowering alcohol

1. Anne Valdespino, "What Would Jesus Drink? Experts Guess What Wine Was Like in Ancient Times and What Modern Ones Are Similar," *Orange County Register*, April 2, 2015, https://www.ocregister.com/2015/04/02/what-would-jesus-drink-experts-guess-what-wine-was-like-in-ancient-times-and-what-modern-ones-are-similar/.
2. Keith Beavers, "What Wine Would Jesus Drink?," *VinePair*, April 11, 2017, https://vinepair.com/wine-geekly/what-wine-would-jesus-drink/#:~:text=So%20wines%20at%20the%20time,you%20didn't%20do%20so.
3. Valdespino, "What Would Jesus Drink?"

content, but it's also possible that the actual drink itself, when mixed, ended up more diluted than our current table red, and certainly more diluted than spirits or high-gravity beers.

The story of the wedding at Cana isn't about wine as wine; it's about the riches of celebration and ensuring that the banquet blesses everyone. It's about having a rare thing and, just when you think you might run out, receiving more of it. We can often imagine God's love as being scarce, so we need to be reminded of the abundance of love offered to us. The wedding at Cana is also about hospitality, always having a way to honor the people in our presence. Given my experiences at various gatherings, the more likely scenario is not that we might run out of alcohol but that there would be nothing delicious and nonalcoholic available to begin with. Imagine a party where the host goes out and gets some zero proof spirits, tonic, and garnish to honor the guest in their home who isn't drinking. That would be miraculous.

During the Last Supper, Jesus drinks wine, but we have every reason to believe it was peasant's wine. Kitty Morse, author of *A Biblical Feast: Foods from the Holy Land,* says this of peasant's wine: "They were happy if it fermented and if it cured some ailments."[4] Doesn't sound like the chef's finest.

We also have plenty of images in Scripture that, if we choose to look at them, show a culture in which people struggled in their relationships with alcohol, just as our own culture struggles, such as Proverbs 23:29–35:

> Who has woe? Who has sorrow?
> Who has strife? Who has complaining?

4. Quoted in Valdespino, "What Would Jesus Drink?"

Who has wounds without cause?
  Who has redness of eyes?
Those who linger late over wine,
  those who keep trying mixed wines.
Do not look at wine when it is red,
  when it sparkles in the cup
  and goes down smoothly.
At the last it bites like a serpent,
  and stings like an adder.
Your eyes will see strange things,
  and your mind utter perverse things.
You will be like one who lies down in the midst
    of the sea,
  like one who lies on the top of a mast.
"They struck me," you will say, "but I was not hurt;
  they beat me, but I did not feel it.
When shall I awake?
  I will seek another drink."

Proverbs 23 warns that alcohol tends to entice us with promises of a good night, then leave us high and dry at daybreak when our bank accounts and text messages tell a story of a good night gone wrong. Sobriety and mindful drinking, on the other hand, don't have to make a big promise, as they just vow to keep us inside our minds, bodies, and souls. Our decisions are made from the seat of our truth, so at daybreak we awaken to the memory that we never abandoned ourselves. Mindfulness around alcohol helps us remain faithful to ourselves, and what we often find in daybreak is that the vow remains faithful to us.

In this same spirit, Proverbs offers a profound look at the illusory positivity of alcohol. The wine that sparkles in the cup brings to mind that, for people who struggle with alcohol, the first drink is the one that sounds appealing, but changing our relationship with alcohol requires remembering the result of the last drink; we have to remember any redness of eyes, any woe, any sorrow. Proverbs speaks of wine as deceptive, equated with the serpent: that ancient image of opposition to God born out of the belief that we know better for ourselves than God knows for us. If we bring mindfulness into how we drink, one shift is to simply look at the whole picture—the first drink, sparkling in the cup, but then all the rest of the drinks. We choose to look into the redness of our eyes, we recognize the moments that felt like a serpent's bite, we give ourselves space to process the perverse thoughts, and we put our finger on the pulse of why we might face the woe and the sorrow but still awaken to seek another drink.

Another biblical passage worthy of our attention is the gospel for the feast of Pentecost. Acts describes the presence of the Holy Spirit as a veritable undoing of Babel, as the scattered voices of difference are intelligible to one another through the Spirit. However, as it happens, divine clarity causes human confusion, and some sneer and assume that those gathered are drunk. I grieve the extent to which this passage elicits so many bad jokes about drunkenness. Imagine: we have the opportunity to celebrate the overwhelming revelation of God, but we choose to make a joke about alcohol. What a loss we face when, given the opportunity to recognize the hope and healing possible through the power of the Holy Spirit, we refuse to grieve the 385 souls who die daily in the United States alone from alcohol-related causes, not to mention how we fail the families grieving those deaths who might have sought out a spiritual community because they are in dire need of their own hope and healing.[5]

Instead of making light of suffering, Pentecost invites us to recognize the difference between the world's understanding of joy and the revelation of the character of the Spirit. How sad that we have the chance to receive the intense and beautiful presence of the Spirit—tongues of fire speaking truth, love, and liberation—but instead we respond to it by dousing it with alcohol, turning ourselves away from healing and hope as the alcohol stokes the flames of our heartache, the emotions we'd rather keep tempered, and the challenges we've been coping with against all odds. We could show up to our spiritual communities with tongues of fire and the revelation of the Holy Spirit to lead us into healing, but alcohol seems to rule the day no matter how we are gathering: at parties for marriages, during celebrations in any form, when we try to build community, when we seek a bonding agent in relationships, when we gather in vocational communities, and so forth.

No, the disciples at Pentecost are not drunk at nine in the morning; they are present to the Spirit who asks that all of us might tend to the blaze, staying inside the presence of the Spirit and trusting that we can boldly proclaim healing from our flamed tongues because we are held within the joy that is equal parts terror and amazement.

Any interpretation of Scripture must acknowledge the world behind the text, the world of the text, and the world in front of the text. The world behind the text helps us understand wine as a beverage safe to drink in a world without

---

5. "Alcohol Abuse Statistics," National Center for Drug Abuse Statistics, July 2021, https://drugabusestatistics.org/alcohol-abuse-statistics/.

water purification systems, and it helps us understand how seasonally wine could become quite scarce. The world revealed in the text invites us into something deeper than getting drunk, whether it's the abundance of God shown through hospitality, a warning against giving in to the deception of alcohol, or a reminder that we are wise not to confuse the activity and presence of the Spirit with something as numbing and distancing as drunkenness. The world in front of the text invites us into a faithful reading of the text, which shows that these Scriptures come from a world where Instacart wasn't dropping off a case of wine at the disciples' front door, where people weren't driving cars that become more deadly when the driver has been drinking. Proverbs helps us recognize that the Bible comes out of a culture that knew how alcohol can threaten our wholeness in mind, body, and soul. How much more, then, should we be concerned about this threat in a world where alcohol is much more widely available?

Sobriety and the Sacred

Sobriety has changed how I understand my relationship to a sacramental life. Sacraments in the church are reminders of the sacred, the hallowed, the existence of the consecrated among the profane, because they are somehow shown to us and also imbued with mystery. Nothing has invited me into a palpable sense of holiness more than sobriety, through which I notice the sacred in every day. My life feels consecrated, as if I received a new ordination after already being ordained twice, because I am newly vested with the promise that God is calling me into a way of living that will bear witness to, and point toward, every way I have received salvation—not by the merits of my sobriety but because I exist as someone who has both died and lived.

In the World Health Organization's global status report on alcohol and health, the first line is important: "Alcohol use is part of many cultural, religious and social practices, and provides perceived pleasure to many users. This new report shows the other side of alcohol: the lives its harmful use claims, the diseases it triggers, the violence and injuries it causes, and the pain and suffering endured as a result."[6] We know religion wields power and influences how we live our lives, so religious communities must take note of their calling to nourish the souls of the creatures of God and reduce the harm religion's power and influence might cause. Part of this involves scrutinizing how we have connected alcohol and spirituality. If we look at how we are doing as a people, both spiritually and more generally, examining with honesty how our rituals and actions show what we believe—y'all, we are not well, and alcohol isn't healing us. We don't have to be churchy to look into this and see that this is a spiritual challenge, because it disconnects us from the true community and communion we were created to receive. We are wired for connection, but then we celebrate this connection through the act of disconnecting from ourselves and others through alcohol, so we become a people with discordant beliefs and rituals, putting ourselves in the midst of this present spiritual crisis.

If we, as a people, can fight past the hangover of alcohol culture and begin to recognize the gulf between us and our

6. "Global Status Report on Alcohol and Health 2018," World Health Organization, September 27, 2018, https://www.who.int/publications/i/item/97892 41565639.

joy, we can at least start the process of figuring out the way across. If this sounds dire, remember that any chance our world has to be delivered into true freedom begins with dire circumstances that, against all odds, place us right here, in this exact place, which looks like bad news before it is good news—the holy ground where revelation and resurrection promise to meet us.

Alcohol is, among other things, an opportunity to escape but never move, to not feel what is in front of us. Alcohol is an escape hatch, but at the bottom of it, we tend to find the problems that forced us to cope. Coping with alcohol keeps us in feedback loops, such that because we tried to escape our hurt, we stay in our hurt. When we get mindful about our alcohol use, the question becomes, is this way of coping helping us to heal? To change how we cope, we have to add new coping mechanisms that allow us to stay just a little bit longer in the hurt. Staying present through coping differently allows us to feel the feeling so that it can pass, and in letting the feeling pass, we aren't staying in the feedback loop. Ironically, escaping holds us in our pain, and staying with the feeling, even just for a minute longer than we're used to, helps us leave it. Whatever moment you are in, you can be only in this moment, and the Spirit who plumbs the depths of the Pit to bring life to those who are in death knows how to find you. We don't have to be like those who are without hope, because if we stay, we will be found, and then we can be delivered.

If sacraments and rituals give us a present, tangible way to be in communion with God, they must actually speak to the present, tangible realities of the human condition. Those present, tangible realities include the global death toll of more than three million souls annually due to alcohol consumption, cementing how ignorance of the risks and promotion of alcohol regardless of the risks are an obvious participation in death, not any sort of spiritual gift.[7] What good is an invitation to the great banquet feast of God if our jokes about the contents of the chalice take away the joy we sought in this blessed Communion? What good is the overwhelming belief that Communion joins us as one Body across time and space when we have made the sacramental wine such an idol that instead of connecting us to the saints, it distances us from them?

It makes sense that we find hope in the idea of a banquet feast awaiting us on the other side of death, but if all we care about is the fact that it's supposedly filled with well-aged wines, I'll pass. The consistent interpretation that a huge party full of wine should be something I look forward to when I die creates an undesirable heaven. The unity with God I have always desired when receiving Communion is what I still desire from it, but now I find union with God in sobriety and not in a chalice of wine. Overreliance on the belief that union with God comes through a depressant leaves me wondering whether there is anything sacred in the rite, because the depressive effects of alcohol didn't help me feel the true presence of God, only true distance from God. As Rowan Williams writes in *Resurrection*, "The sacramental act identifies the Church, the whole community, by articulating where it is that the Church looks for the sources of its life and understanding: it is a sort of 'taking cognizance' of why the Church strives to live thus and not otherwise.

7. "Alcohol," World Health Organization, July 2021, https://www.who.int/health-topics/alcohol#tab=tab_1.

It allows the source-event, the mystery of cross and resurrection, to become present again."[8] We must preside over sacraments that display cognizance of how we live, why we live in alcohol culture and not otherwise. We are called to ask ourselves what the source of our life and understanding actually reflects.

You might be thinking that Communion doesn't represent the heavy drinking that would distance us from God. But our beliefs, rituals, and prayers are interconnected, and in spiritual communities that use wine as a sacrament, there is often a corresponding alcohol culture. If there is to be anything sacred in the rite, spiritual communities and individuals alike must practice mindfulness around how our ritual of elevating a glass of wine and saying it is God has shaped our belief that alcohol is more worthy of our adoration than the souls whose lives have come to an end in that same chalice. Spiritual communities must practice mindfulness around alcohol not to condemn the sacraments but to reflect on why the sacraments exist: to draw us close to God.

We can look to communities who celebrate Communion without involving wine at all: plenty of denominations use grape juice for the sacrament. Modern liturgical shops sell mustum, also called mustum grape juice, to be used for Communion. Mustum comes from the crushed-up grapes and their juice before they are fermented to become wine. In Jesus's time, commoners (who typically used wine for survival, not social engagements) needed wine to last until the next harvest, so the mustum was added to stop fermentation. Often, sacramental communities are passionate about the

8. Rowan Williams, *Resurrection: Interpreting the Easter Gospel* (Cleveland: Pilgrim, 2003), 52.

drama of the sacraments, attempting to enact rituals that reflect what we know about the rituals historically. The use of mustum participates in this love for history beautifully because mustum is a beverage, like wine, that was shared during Jesus's time. Using mustum would connect us to our history and bring us closer to enacting rituals that are hospitable to people who don't drink.

Additionally, just as it has become customary for sacramental communities to offer gluten-free Communion bread or wafers, it must become customary for sacramental communities to offer nonalcoholic options in recognition of the health risks caused by alcohol. Additionally, theological understanding of Communion must face the greater question of why it is necessary to keep using alcohol given that there are nonalcoholic options available and this sacrament isn't a wine-tasting event, especially as we confront how our practices have elevated wine to being so important that it poses a danger to us. Ideally, spiritual rituals would actually become an inclusive experience through which all of creation is welcomed into the true presence of God, so that our worship could become the banquet feast we seek.

Theologians spend years, pages upon pages, proclaiming the importance of the sacraments, how what we do matters, and the beauty of what we are saying about God in our holy liturgies. I'm not interested in throwing out these holy practices, but I am committed to calling spiritual communities to a change of heart about how we understand ourselves in relation to alcohol. I'm obviously part of a church that uses wine, and I've witnessed the energy, intentionality, and prayer we have put into the theology and practice of these rituals. If we profess to be a people of resurrection, we must put the same amount of energy, intentionality, and prayer into the theology and practice of how our relationship with alcohol affects beloved children of God and their flourishing. We must reckon with how all our practices around alcohol, both inside and outside the sacrament, can prevent bearers of the image of God from fostering the spirit of thanksgiving we intend to offer them.

As a recovery coach, priest, and spiritual director, I'm often approached by people struggling with alcohol and with how it has affected their faith. Time and time again I learn that others are dealing with what I faced when I got sober: trying to change how they drink or get sober, all the while trying to hide it from their church because church feels like an unsafe place to share that part of their lives. Any drinking community that refuses to become mindful about the role alcohol plays in its members' lives will remain a place where people get secretly sober out of fear, and because of this, we will keep missing the chance to witness the beauty of their resurrections. (And make no mistake: this is the community's loss.) If our rituals in which we claim to see God through the vessel of wine are to be offered with any integrity, we must be willing to see God both in the chalice and in the ninety-nine thousand souls who died in 2020 due to alcohol-related causes in the United States alone.[9] I pray that as we welcome the world to the banquet feast, proclaiming that our table stretches wide enough for all to come and be made well, we would offer bread to the hungry without simultaneously building a roadblock to prevent some from receiving the healing they seek.

9. Roni Caryn Rabin, "Alcohol-Related Deaths Spiked during the Pandemic, a Study Shows," *New York Times*, March 22, 2022, https://www.nytimes.com/2022/03/22/health/alcohol-deaths-covid.html.

refresh and reflect

Take this opportunity to think about the role alcohol might play in your spirituality.

- How have interpretations of sacred texts influenced your thoughts on alcohol?
- If alcohol is part of your spiritual rituals, how do these rituals with alcohol offer you meaning? Can you imagine these rituals holding meaning without alcohol?
- What is the most central message you wish to receive in your spiritual community's worship?

alcohol and trauma

Showing Ourselves Compassion as We Ask Why We Drink

WHEN I STARTED to examine my drinking, no one had introduced me to the idea that my patterns may not be my own failure but a condition of how so many of us have been programmed to drink, think, and feel. I also wasn't hitting "rock bottom" as I imagined it, so I didn't know how to give my drinking some space to breathe or myself some time for further reflection. I thought I was completely alone.

I read through the Big Book from Alcoholics Anonymous (AA). It is, understandably, a place where many of us start, because AA is arguably the most widespread recovery community we have, and countless people have experienced healing through its fellowship. Every church I could think of hosted AA meetings, and I already owned the Big Book because I had read it in seminary. I knew enough about AA and its twelve steps to turn to it as I explored how it might answer some of my questions, but I just couldn't connect. And yet I struggled to see any other entry points into changing my drinking, so . . . I just kept drinking the way I always had. I needed a way forward that didn't make me promise sobriety, since I didn't know whether sobriety was my path. When I first recognized I didn't like how I drank, I pondered my options. The response felt clear: sobriety or bust. With limited options and lack of clarity about whether sobriety felt possible, I was sent straight back to the bottle, feeling somehow lonelier.

Looking back, I wonder whether my sober journey would have begun years earlier had I found sober spaces where I felt more care and openness to sober curiosity that didn't have a specific agenda. I needed sober spaces open to the idea that a person might not be ready to quit but might still be ready to safely question their drinking, secure in the knowledge they would be loved regardless of where prayer and discernment led them. I wonder what my life would have become if my spiritual communities had known how to love me in that tender space, the space I kept secret from them because the church always poured me another round. I did finally find ways forward—outside of the religious realm, mind you—but it took years to get there. This, however, gave me my new life's journey of trying to offer that care and openness as early as possible to anyone with that first inkling.

Why Do We Drink?

When I meet with a recovery coaching client for the first time, I ask for a brief history of their relationship with alcohol. I listen for the narratives inside a person's drinking history. Narratives tell me how a person understands the importance of drinking in their lives, how alcohol has been used, and the messages that undergird how they drink. Many of the same narratives pop up frequently: drinking to fit in, drinking to try to build community, the idea that drinking is a part of who they are, and drinking to cope with stress or trauma. We have to reckon with how these narratives are interwoven with drinking, because they invite us to remember how we have created a false binary between those who drink and those who "have a problem." A healthier and more compassionate reaction is to notice these pervasive narratives and how they are part of the lives of many different people who drink, regardless of how they drink. We can break down the binary and see in other people some of our own narratives, which joins us to one another in a common challenge without making any individual the "problem drinker."

My drinking history speaks to how trauma can change a relationship with alcohol. I was a social drinker, sometimes overdoing it in communal settings, and then I tried to cut back when I started my first job. However, later I experienced trauma and couldn't escape the overwhelming feeling that I wasn't safe, even in my own home. The lack of safety, coupled with other stressors, led to me, like clockwork, cracking open a bottle of wine at the end of a long day. I would cross the threshold into my home and struggle with the effect of trauma on my mind, body, and soul. Homes are thought of as "safe havens," but if violated, homes can become triggers. As I began to heal from trauma (a lifelong process, but I was getting better), my drinking didn't change, because it had become a pattern. Our bodies don't differentiate between patterns we end up in situationally and habits we intend to take on for life, so even if we can change the stimuli, the ingrained pattern can then become the trigger. I wasn't coming home to a physical space being the trigger, but now the cue was simply coming home. A person can get out of a triggering situation and discover that their cues and triggers have adapted because of patterns developed over time, even when they have been working hard to try to heal.

My recovery coaching practice is founded on the truth that coping is normal. Coping is not something to be ashamed of; coping is an inevitability of being alive. Everyone faces realities that require coping, and how we cope depends on many factors. We have to acknowledge the factors that are not in our control: class, race, genetics, family of origin, trauma history, the state of our mental health, the state of our physical health, disability, access to health care, responsibilities entrusted to us, and much more.

When I look back at my heaviest drinking days, the days of the deep trauma and the intensive therapy I went through to try to heal, I know that drinking was how I was surviving, and on my best days I don't fault myself for staying alive. If you are struggling with alcohol, you are likely trying to survive. Changing how we drink is the work of recognizing how we are coping, asking ourselves whether drinking is helping us heal, and honoring the factors that challenge our coping. It's not about demonizing your current coping but about adding new coping mechanisms into the mix so that we can cope in a way that truly leads toward healing.

This is part of why we have to change dominant narratives around drinking. It's considered normal for friends to take you out drinking after a breakup, normal to go on the "Olivia

Pope diet" of wine and popcorn, normal to own a wine glass that fits an entire bottle so you can say "I only had one glass," as the memes proclaim. But when trauma is added to the mix, this way of coping (whether it is coping with a breakup, with the stressors of an intense job, or with loneliness) will place more stress on our nervous system. The mixture of a person facing trauma, or even just the daily challenges of being alive, with the messages that drinking away problems and stressors is "just the way things are" causes harm while a person is already struggling. Asking for help is always an exercise in vulnerability to some degree, but we have heaped so much judgment and stigma onto this specific part of our lives that our vulnerability is heightened. In an ideal world, changing our relationship with alcohol would be as commonplace and acceptable as any other dietary choice we make.

Understanding Trauma

Our relationship with alcohol is connected to trauma—both in a communal and individual sense. Traumatic events in an individual's life leave them needing to cope. Trauma is an open wound in search of closure and is marked by how it returns, which is a return fueled by "an inability to fully process an event."[1] This return includes "persistent intrusive and distressing images of recollections of the traumatic event."[2] Trauma disrupts our lives, creating the "enigma of what remains" defined by "alterations in time, body, and word."[3]

1. Shelly Rambo, *Spirit and Trauma: A Theology of Remaining* (Louisville: Westminster John Knox, 2010), 7.
2. Rambo, *Spirit and Trauma*, 18.
3. Rambo, *Spirit and Trauma*, 7, 18.

Much of the suffering related to trauma comes from the root of the missed event, the event left unprocessed. The pain is located in the gap, such that "the suffering does not solely lie in the violence of trauma's impact (in its happening) but in the ways in which that happening, that occurrence, was not known or grasped at that time."[4]

Trauma can rupture our relationships, with ourselves and others, and keep us from dreaming about a different future because so much of our energy is given toward protection and survival. Returning to the experience of that pain illuminates why a person coping with trauma might self-medicate through substances to try to escape the return. The more we understand trauma and the pain it causes, the more we can grow in compassion.

A mindless relationship with alcohol can itself take on the shape of trauma, because a problematic relationship with drinking often exists as an open wound in search of closure. Problematic drinking includes returns to using in a way we don't like, defined by an inability to fully process the event of the drinking and its aftermath. We then face anxiety and depression either brought on by or exacerbated by alcohol, resulting in intrusive and distressing memories of our drinking or in shame about the memories we don't have. We keep facing the distressing recollections, but without the ability to fully process the event. Alcohol, like trauma, can begin to disrupt our lives and our relationships, with ourselves and others, and it can keep us from imagining a future. In the aftermath of the drinking event, the recollections, any repercussions of our drinking, and the burden of shame, mean

4. Rambo, *Spirit and Trauma*, 20.

a tremendous amount of energy is given toward protection and survival.

In *Recovery from Trauma, Addiction, or Both: Strategies for Finding Your Best Self*, Lisa M. Najavits notes that trauma and addiction create a comorbidity that can result in a "downward spiral or toxic feedback loop." But their link to one another also provides a source of healing, because "improving one can help the other in an upward spiral."[5] While we might have participated in the downward spiral, we can also participate in helping others, and ourselves, recover from trauma and addiction. As Shelly Rambo posits, "The good news lies in the ability of Christian theology to witness between life and death, in its ability to forge a new discourse between the two."[6] The new discourse around alcohol forged between life and death looks like escaping not our lives but cycles of self-harm around alcohol through fully processing the events of our drinking, which serves as a way for us to exist more joyfully in this middle place. When we take on practices of healing around alcohol, we don't suddenly escape the middle place of death and life indicative of being in this world, but we do learn how to tell the truth in this middle place.

The invitation to change our relationship with alcohol is a search for a true profession of faith. This is the truth that is bad news before it is good news, but it never suggests that you or anyone else are bad news. No, this truth loves us with compassion and acknowledges that, if we are mindlessly drinking, we are probably avoiding an awareness of the harm alcohol causes because we have experienced trauma or are

5. Lisa M. Najavits, *Recovery from Trauma, Addiction, or Both: Strategies for Finding Your Best Self* (New York: Guilford, 2017), 107.
6. Rambo, *Spirit and Trauma*, 8.

in a state of trauma with drinking. We, then, are invited to take on a new posture of healing in light of this knowledge, which provides the courage needed to reckon with all the good and all the bad and then create a sacred middle place of joyfulness.

Healing from Moral Injury

Moral injury is a "strong cognitive and emotional response that can occur following events that violate a person's moral or ethical code," and these events can include acts of commission or omission.[7] In short, it is an experience in which a person feels as though they, through no fault of their own or because of difficult circumstances, acted in a way outside their values or didn't act when they should have. Moral injury happens when we don't intend to cause harm but we do nonetheless.

My friend David Peters was in a car wreck when he was a freshman in college; he lived and others died, which is a burden he still carries even though he did not intend harm. Peters, who is a priest, veteran, and military chaplain, has written about his experience. He helps us understand the difference between moral injury and post-traumatic stress disorder (PTSD): "If PTSD results from being the prey—re-experiencing the feeling that something is hunting you, hurting you, trying to kill you—then moral injury results from being the predator—where you have done things to hurt people."[8] Moral

7. Victoria Williamson et al., "Moral Injury: The Effect on Mental Health and Implications for Treatment," *The Lancet* 8, no. 6 (2021): 453–55, https://doi.org /10.1016/S2215-0366(21)00113-9.

8. David Peters, "When War Lives On inside You," *Sojourners*, March 2020, https://sojo.net/magazine/march-2020/when-war-lives-inside-you.

injury is an experience of events that can "cause profound feelings of shame and guilt, and alterations in cognitions and beliefs," often accompanied by challenges with coping, such as social difficulty, struggling with substances, and self-harm.[9]

I believe that many of us reckon with some sort of moral injury. One step in spiritual healing regarding alcohol is to recognize how we might be in a state of moral injury because of alcohol. When we look at our relationship with alcohol, both how we have behaved personally and how we have communally ignored its harm, we might experience a sense that we have violated our morals or ethics. We might struggle with things we did while drinking that felt disconnected from our morals. We might feel that we have acted outside our values in some way, whether intentionally or not, or we might feel ashamed of not being better advocates for those who suffer. In our individual drinking, maybe we did things we don't even remember, but later we found out they caused harm. As communities, we have known that addiction is around us, but we often focus on other concerns instead. These are not intentional acts of harm, but they harm just the same, leading us into moral injury.

There is hope in healing from moral injury through "self-forgiveness, acceptance, self-compassion, and (if possible) making amends," which are practices already found in spiritual communities and recovery communities alike.[10] Our spirituality—though our transgressions against it might have given us the moral injury in the first place—becomes the way of healing. Right now, there is no validated treatment for moral injury, but moral injury, challenging

9. Williamson et al., "Moral Injury," 453–55.
10. Williamson et al., "Moral Injury," 453–55.

relationships with substances, and the ever-unfolding nature of trauma are spiritual wounds, and spiritual communities are the ideal place for this healing to find a home. If we wish to build the home, we can't house anyone else's treatment if we don't first admit we need a hospital bed. If we confess to spiritual harm caused by mindless relationships with alcohol, both as individuals and as communities, this act of repentance could create strong bonds between healing from trauma, recovery from substance use, and spirituality.

Imagine a world in which we laid claim to the universality of our pain, our coping, our trauma, our injury, our addiction, and in which we became one spiritual community built on self-forgiveness, acceptance, and self-compassion. The path into this healing from alcohol ultimately would serve as a reunification with the Spirit, as we are invited into harmony with God, ourselves, and our neighbors. Let us go down a path of healing that honors our trauma, loves us in our challenges with coping, and speaks belovedness over our moral injury and absolution over all our mistakes. What an honor it would be if we, spiritual people and communities, could unite past stigma and silence to create a home for souls to heal in the sacred middle place: healing for bodies that hate how they drink but don't know whether they want to quit, healing for hearts reliving the trauma they now call their first moment of death, healing for minds remembering an event they'd give anything to forget. Our joy is made complete when we take our place on the sacred ground that is not just a middle place but a thin place, a holy mixture of remaining within the reality of death and remaining within the profundity of resurrection.

Healing in Spiritual Communities

Communities that continue promoting alcohol use are contributing to hurting others on a soul level. It isn't always a sin of commission but often a sin of omission, yet it all perpetuates a system of harm toward God's creation. This is why spiritual communities with this norm should seek amendment of heart.

Spiritual communities should be the safest places for sober people or people who are being mindful about their drinking. When people choose to cast off their favorite way to numb themselves and instead choose to awaken to themselves, they should be as welcomed by their communities as they are by the Spirit who receives them into arms of mercy. What if the relationship between sin and alcohol isn't that individuals are moral failures but that spiritual communities promoting harmful practices and mentalities, or ignoring their impact, are called to take on the role of the penitent? For spiritual communities to lead the charge in changing drinking culture, we must also give space for individual care around the way we drink, because if we try to change our culture without first changing our hearts, we might end up back in an identity conflict partnered with not enough coping skills. If our spiritual communities and the people in them wish to thrive in mind, body, and soul, we will have to bring mindfulness into alcohol use at the individual and communal level.

I believe our best way forward is not by forcing spiritual communities to feel shame but instead by inviting them to confession and absolution. Again, if you're part of a spiritual community that has participated in promoting alcohol use, rather than hearing this as a reason to spiral into self-hatred and condemnation, try to receive it as an insight into how this is a distance between your community and God, a distance between your community and the people in recovery who are maybe seeking you as their spiritual home. Receive this word as a calling into a closeness to God *that is accessible to our communities through healing.* Plus, if you are in a community with an alcohol culture, remember this: addiction is a search for healing; your people are hurting. Naming an alcohol culture is good for everyone, because it surfaces the deep hurting so that we can offer healing. If we name the distance, we can begin to bridge the gap. Though not all spiritual people hold to specific practices of repentance, we can gather the import of asking for forgiveness as it is present in a variety of belief systems, such as the rite of reconciliation of the penitent in some Christian traditions, the AA practice of making amends, Judaism's practice of *teshuva* and Yom Kippur, and the Muslim belief that forgiveness is inseparably bound to peace.

We Cannot Go Back . . .

In early sobriety, I was sitting at my desk in my office when I was hit with the memory of something I had done when I was drunk. I hadn't realized how difficult it would be to face these memories, especially without being numb to them. I had given up the quickest way to avoid an emotion (pouring a glass of wine), which meant I had to sit in the memories and feel whatever feelings they evoked, which was (and still is) usually shame. And, y'all, it sucks. I remember thinking: I got sober and instead of a grand prize all I got was *the full unmitigated force of shame.*

Still, I learned, it felt better to feel feelings than to shove them down. One of the most important things I have learned about navigating shame from St. Brené Brown is this: tell shame to get the hell out of here. Don't run from the emotion (well, you can't; you're sober), but also, don't let shame sit beside you. The whole time I was trying to quit, quitting, drinking again, trying again, then finally quitting for good, I started gathering one-line prayers I could call on to shift my inner narrative. They were, and still are, how I tell shame to get the hell out of here. I tried to say them to myself, even though I thought it was ridiculous. The idea was that if I started giving my brain some other messages, not just messages of self-hatred, I could start the lifelong process of changing my self-talk. I rolled my eyes when I first started but felt just desperate enough to try anything.

Here's the deal: it was bullshit until it worked. It worked that day at my desk, and to this day, when shame tries to hang out and show me a memory of me doing something dumb when I was drunk—playing on a loop like the world's worst TikTok—I present my eviction notice. With my hand on my heart, I prayed then and I pray now: "I cannot go back, but I can move forward differently."

Only in the years that have passed have I seen how this simple prayer holds within it the shape of confession. If our spiritual community has promoted destructive understandings of alcohol, heaping shame on ourselves won't change the behavior; if anything, doling out shame will promise that the behaviors stay, because shame immobilizes us. We have to tell shame to get the hell out of here and instead pursue a practice of confession, acknowledging that we can't go back but we can move forward differently. We can confess our past, and instead of sitting in the shame of it, we can receive absolution and hear comforting words: we can release the heavy burdens of how we have participated in this challenge and be refreshed by God through absolution. We can trust in this forgiveness and how it will lead our community into everlasting life through amendment of heart.

Addressing how spiritual communities have participated in promoting alcohol culture with a model of confession as our way forward allows us to name the problem and take a new approach. Changing our communities is shared work; none of us bears the burden alone, which is a comfort. We can renounce shame through accountability. Forgiveness is, at its core, a shift in identity, the invitation to somehow exist as we are and become a new creation at the same time. We can receive these comforting words as a reminder: when God looks at us to see who we are, God does not see our offenses; God looks into our souls and calls us beloved.

Practicing forgiveness does not justify what we have done or justify how others have harmed us. Every way of forgiveness, whether it's within a community, toward someone else, or toward ourselves, is a practice that offers healing. All we can do is choose to not go back and to move forward differently. To change alcohol culture, we must become convinced we can be forgiven in our own actions and for the mistakes of our communities so that our future isn't defined by our past. Whether you are reading this with guilt from the cultural impact of your actions or as a sober person who can barely stand up when you are reminded of your past, may you hear the words of absolution: you are forgiven. You can unbind yourself from the yoke of what you did when you were drinking; you can be freed from the burdens of how you have caused harm against yourself and others. There is rejoicing, for you were lost and are now found; you were dead and are now alive. You are forgiven; now you can move forward differently.

We do not have to keep starting over. Beginnings are beautiful, but inside grace, new beginnings are less like starting over and more like remembering the promise of divine love we forgot when we experienced a pain so grievous we dared to ask whether God would be faithful to the promise. God has all the time in the world, eternity in a single breath, and God chooses to spend it waiting for us, waiting with us, preceding us, and following us with grace. Whether or not we can feel it when we stare up at the heavens with curses on our lips as prayers, we are never far from the Spirit. We don't have to stay in the far-off places where shame sent us; we can come home to the Spirit who is forever waiting for us. When we struggle with the confession part, the absolution part, the "How do I move forward differently?" question, remember, beloved: even in those far-off places, God is somehow both beside us in the places we imagine God would never go and back home readying a banquet feast for our return. We can always come home.

As a recovery coach, I find that people often choose to work with me because their history with church was a trigger for them to drink and they trust me to help them navigate that specific part of their path as they change their relationship with alcohol. As a spiritual director, I find that people often choose to work with me because their sobriety, or tumultuous relationship with alcohol, has affected their spirituality and they want to work with someone who can understand the spiritual impact of both drinking and quitting. The list of ways spiritual institutions have neglected to let their professed beliefs call them into intentionality around alcohol is, in my world, forever unfurling.

... But We Can Move Forward Differently

The same way I came alive in sobriety, our whole culture can awaken to a new way of being. The first step is to let go of how we have blurred the lines between our identity as the faithful and our identity as people who drink, an awakening made possible through confession and reconciliation. Rowan Williams illuminates the power we can have within spiritual communities, *especially* sacramental communities, if we are willing to be a culture that "identifies itself as oppressor and traitor, yet also the penitent and restored kin in Christ." We can actually become who we are called to be through forgiveness and communion: "the Easter community, guilty and restored, the gathering of those whose identity is defined by their new relation to Jesus crucified and raised, who identify themselves as forgiven."[11]

Lest you think I am somehow officiating this confession and not participating in it, I am praying: "Go in peace, and pray for me, a sinner." I didn't come to these conclusions about changing the disastrous wedding of alcohol with spirituality from the outside looking in; I arrived by way of my own confession of sin and as I continue to wrestle with my participation in promoting alcohol culture when I drank, especially as a priest. One of the hardest reckonings I face is how I was not hospitable to sober people; when I drank, I perpetuated the norms that harm the creatures of God, and

11. Rowan Williams, *Resurrection: Interpreting the Easter Gospel* (Cleveland: Pilgrim, 2003), 51–52.

I lived in opposition to my own beliefs. I work hard to practice self-forgiveness, but those practices are as lifelong as spirituality and sobriety. Still, we can each pray that one-line prayer and let it draw our souls and our spiritual communities into confession: "I cannot go back, but I can move forward differently." I know the prayer works because I prayed it earlier today.

refresh and reflect

If it feels possible for you, take some time to name your traumas, the wounds you have tended, the ways you have survived. In naming them, honor how you have survived and the strength you possess, and try to release any self-judgment about the ways you have needed to cope. Throughout the next few weeks, if you begin to judge yourself for the ways you have needed to cope, try to stop, place your hand on your heart, close your eyes, and pray: "I cannot go back, but I can move forward differently."

reading the big book with a box of chardonnay

Moving Past False Binaries on Our Path to Healing

I DIDN'T QUIT COLD TURKEY, and many don't. I spent years trying to get sober. I had interior doubts, but the curiosities about whether I wanted to quit were always pushed down by another round. I remember doing Whole30 once, but I like to call it my "Whole28" because I got invited to a party on the twenty-eighth day and I don't handle temptation well. It wasn't an intentional attempt at quitting, but in retrospect I realize it was a way of trying to cut back. The experiment backfired because I was then able to say, "Of course I don't have a problem; I didn't drink for twenty-eight days! People who don't drink for twenty-eight days are fine."

At the time I couldn't have known that the question wasn't, "Do I have a problem?" but instead, "Is my life joyful?" So I kept drinking. Cognitive dissonance reigned.

One turning point would come years later, when I learned that a friend of mine had quit drinking. In too many ways she was, well, like me. Cognitive dissonance had always given me options to get out of this situation before—"they are not like me, thus their situation is different and doesn't mean I should change anything." But cognitive dissonance fell silent in the wake of my friend's truth. While I allowed myself to entertain sober curiosity more than I ever had before, it was still so impossibly big that I did what any English major would do: I got a bunch of books. I bought them on Kindle so they were hidden in my phone, because I feared anyone seeing me with a book about recovery. Quit lit: the new scarlet letter.

I didn't quit drinking—I didn't even cut back!—but I started to heal. I would come home after dinner and drinks and grab a book before bed, but I started grabbing sobriety books. I read the Alcoholics Anonymous Big Book with a box of chardonnay, spilling wine and the occasional gin and tonic on its pages. My marginalia ink blurred in the spilling, revealing prayers from a soul still figuring out how to live a life where the reflections on the sides of her pages were blurry only because of the mystery of God, not because God felt hidden behind heavy pours.

As I kept moving into deeper wisdom about changing this part of my life, I was given the perfect chance to test-drive sobriety again as a priest: giving up alcohol for Lent! I thought it would give me a foolproof excuse, and I could then just . . . somehow . . . slide into being a full-time sober person. But it did not work that way, and I found myself drinking again on Palm Sunday (it had technically been forty days, and exhibit A will reflect the agreement made per my contract). I had accepted a new job and faced the thing I couldn't bear to do sober: say goodbye. Only weeks later I would move, which held the possibility of a geographical fix.

Once I was resettled, I went to a few dinners at people's homes and other social events, and I didn't drink. I said something very true: alcohol was affecting my migraines; it made my body sick. I had morning rituals, repeated positive affirmations, and gathered positive coping skills. I fed myself a steady diet of the podcast *Armchair Expert* with Dax Shepard and Monica Padman, because listening to people talk about how they also struggled with alcohol helped me feel less alone. The same way my friend's proclamation of sobriety helped me claim it for myself, listening to Shepard and friends tell their stories connected them to me, and in my sober loneliness I felt as though I had some sort of community.

I didn't know what to do with the endless hours of the evenings, when sober loneliness struck hardest, so I started watching as much stand-up comedy as I could. I watched sober comedians like John Mulaney, living for the bits about his sobriety. It felt cathartic and beautiful to listen to people I admired talk about how they faced the same question of sobriety I faced, and in admiring them for their courage, I began to admire myself for mine. Most importantly, I laughed about the question of sobriety, and this made me all the more joyful. I listened to Pete Holmes's podcast *You Made It Weird*, and over time and across many episodes I realized we had been on a similar path of thinking about our drinking, each of us embracing sobriety in our own way. I've always loved comedy, but in the chasm of finding myself I needed and cherished those reasons to laugh—the lifting of my spirits without any spirits.

Eventually I went back to drinking because all the positive affirmations, podcasts, and comedy specials in the world couldn't ransom me from the loneliness I felt in a new place. I didn't know how to build friendships without alcohol. An invitation to dinner sent me back into months of drinking, but unlike any of my previous returns to the bottle, I kept my practices. I continued my positive self-talk, listened to *Armchair Expert* and *You Made It Weird*, and indulged my love of stand-up comedy. I had changed my relationship with alcohol, even though I had gone back to drinking, and I knew it had changed because even with a drink in my hand I could look into the salt-rimmed glass and know I wanted sobriety. I just didn't know how to quit.

The magic of this season is that I now recognize how much going back to drinking helped me get sober. I needed the harsh juxtaposition between what it felt like to wake up for two months without a hangover and the devastating return of the hangover—a pain I had once known as the act of simply waking up. Not to mention the two months of no drinking meant I lost my tolerance, so my drinking experiences felt worse: the booze was harder on my body, and I felt more shame. The harsh juxtaposition was, well, harsh, but when my soul asked me which way I wanted to live—sober or drinking—I was just attentive enough to the Spirit to finally choose loving myself through sobriety and whatever terror and amazement it would contain.

A Long Obedience in the Same Direction

We think of quitting drinking as a one-time decision, but it is better known as a long obedience in the same direction.[1] Some can quit cold turkey, but if that becomes the bar for success, we are in danger of telling people on the path of this long obedience that they don't qualify for the very joy they are moving toward. Deciding you want to quit drinking still means you have to learn how to cross the threshold into a party and, when you cross that threshold again, not have any alcohol in your system. Not drinking takes work, it takes practice, it requires us to embark on a long obedience in the same direction—even if we drink at the party and think the compass must be broken.

The binary of needing to either be completely sober or continue drinking in a way that harms us excludes the many, many people who find themselves in the mysterious in-between—where I first started my long obedience. If we facilitate the conversation about changing relationships with alcohol as needing a definitive start date or requiring a specific path of healing or beholden to a linear passage of time, we will lose people. People will understandably struggle between the desire to change how they drink and the practicality of crossing the threshold a second time sober. The binary of staying stone-cold sober versus harmfully drinking might tell them their "failure" demands choosing one or the other, and damn if we don't tend to choose the devil we know.

We would be wise to recognize how attempts to grow in mindfulness around alcohol are inside healing; they are not

1. Eugene Peterson, *A Long Obedience in the Same Direction: Discipleship in an Instant Society* (Downers Grove, IL: InterVarsity, 2021).

divorced from healing if we don't try "correctly." We will need to honor this fluidity if we desire to see the greatest number of people heal. Now, there are plenty of stories more linear than mine, and I celebrate them just the same. But opening ourselves to honoring how healing doesn't have to be linear (for ourselves and others) can encourage weary souls, helping us all stay obedient to that same direction.

Sobriety is, for so many of us, a progression, an unfolding, an intuitive process of embodiment, and the inkling that a more joyful life is possible. God can speak to us about our relationship with alcohol through this same fluidity, this same unfolding of ourselves over time, this same welcome into a life that feels as though it might lead us away from our dreams while actually leading us into them.

Alcohol Use Disorder

To see how we are evolving in our understanding of relationships with alcohol, we need look no further than the Diagnostic and Statistical Manual of Mental Disorders, fifth edition (DSM-5), a publication from the American Psychiatric Association, which offers comprehensive insight into the diagnosis of mental disorders. In 2013, the DSM-5 changed its definition and insight concerning alcohol use disorder (AUD), as it is formally called. The DSM-5 acknowledges how alcohol use is on a range rather than within a binary of problem drinking versus permissible drinking. The DSM-5 helps us understand our relationship to AUD by asking about our experiences with alcohol over the past year (see the accompanying sidebar). If, over the past year, we have had at least two of the experiences listed on the survey, this means we

Diagnostic Criteria for Alcohol Use Disorder

In the past year, have you:

- Had times when you ended up drinking more, or longer, than you intended?
- More than once wanted to cut down or stop drinking, or tried to, but couldn't?
- Spent a lot of time drinking? Or being sick or getting over other aftereffects?
- Wanted a drink so badly you couldn't think of anything else?
- Found that drinking—or being sick from drinking—often interfered with taking care of your home or family? Or caused job troubles? Or school problems?
- Continued to drink even though it was causing trouble with your family or friends?
- Given up or cut back on activities that were important or interesting to you, or gave you pleasure, in order to drink?
- More than once gotten into situations while or after drinking that increased your chances of getting hurt (such as driving, swimming, using machinery, walking in a dangerous area, or having unsafe sex)?
- Continued to drink even though it was making you feel depressed or anxious or adding to another health problem? Or after having had a memory blackout?
- Had to drink much more than you once did to get the effect you want? Or found that your usual number of drinks had much less effect than before?
- Found that when the effects of alcohol were wearing off, you had withdrawal symptoms, such as trouble sleeping, shakiness, restlessness, nausea, sweating, a racing heart, or a seizure? Or sensed things that were not there?

Source: "Alcohol Use Disorder: A Comparison between DSM–IV and DSM–5," National Institute on Alcohol Abuse and Alcoholism, April 2021, https://www.niaaa.nih.gov/publications/brochures-and-fact-sheets/alcohol-use-disorder-comparison-between-dsm.

are inside the range of AUD, which can be understood as encompassing mild, moderate, and severe cases. You might take a minute to compassionately explore what the survey reveals about your own relationship with alcohol.

Reading through this list might feel terrifying. But it offers some good news because it means we can begin to help people when they are in the mild and moderate stages of AUD rather than waiting to offer support until someone reaches severe AUD. The downside is that all stages of AUD have become normative. This is why bringing mindfulness to our relationship with alcohol is important and no longer relegated to people we would say are "problem drinkers," because, as the list illustrates, many people could have two of the experiences listed and not be thought of as "having a problem" in our society.

If you're struggling with how you see yourself in the list, think of it this way: go watch a movie or show, and assess characters based on the AUD survey. It's not you; it's how we've built a culture that normalizes having AUD, and that's not your fault. You likely weren't encouraged to keep your finger on the pulse of your drinking. Instead, when you went through a horrible breakup and felt the most depressed you'd ever felt at a tender and formative age, someone probably said, "Let's go out for drinks so you can forget them." We all have some agency, but receiving the AUD range with self-hatred does not help us heal.

I hope we can explore this range and begin to love and support people when they are in every stage of AUD. What if awareness of this survey gently invites you to begin the work of changing your relationship with alcohol, whatever that may mean for you? If you look at this survey and answer "yes" to a few of them, maybe more than you are comfortable with, you might be thinking, "This means I have to quit, and that sounds impossible." But what if this just means you could pick a few of the symptoms from the survey that feel most difficult and start to get support regarding them? There are several gifts of understanding AUD as falling within a range: (1) we can see where we are and know if we are escalating, (2) we can recognize the symptoms and begin to work on them, and (3) as we begin to work on these symptoms through mindfulness, we can celebrate if we are de-escalating.

It is common to look at this list and think that none of this is true for you. Part of this is because we adapt, over time, to the norm of how we drink. For instance, it's common for my clients who are changing their relationship with alcohol to realize they don't have any hobbies. Over time they adapted to their evenings being taken up by alcohol and streaming services, or alcohol and phone scrolling, and it isn't until they remove the alcohol that they realize they don't have joyful practices to fill the void. In other words, you may not think you have "given up or cut back on activities that were important or interesting to you or that gave you pleasure in order to drink," but often we adapt to drinking being the activity that is important and interesting, which leads to it becoming a barrier between ourselves and practices that enhance joy, which is a symptom of AUD.

Another example is the symptom of continuing to drink even though it makes you feel depressed or anxious or adds to another health problem. Over time we can adapt to the belief that fill-in-the-blank-with-however-we-feel-right-now is just "normal" depression, anxiety, and bodily discomfort without realizing that those challenges could possibly decrease through decreased drinking. Or imagine this: you drink daily, and every morning you feel a little nauseated and sick to your stomach. You ignore it, because of course you feel that way—you're hung over. When you read the AUD list, your brain avoids discomfort by minimizing your sleep issues, nausea, and racing heart by saying that you have always had a racing heart from anxiety, your insomnia is probably just due to stress, and the nausea is a mild symptom. However, it's very possible that all those experiences are exacerbated by the daily drinking, so it would be helpful to note that the experience relates to AUD.

If that feels too difficult (understandably so), think of it less as a "sign you have AUD" and more as an invitation to put your finger on the pulse of your body. Consider talking to a doctor or other healer about those experiences to try to get to the root, because, if nothing else, I'm sure you'd like to feel better. In the sense of how we care for the body more generally, those symptoms can be linked to other illnesses, and by writing them off as a hangover, you could be precluding a health diagnosis and proper treatment.

One of the most powerful things we can do is to stop perpetuating the idea that there is a line a person must cross to suddenly need help. In spirituality, we don't cross a line when we suddenly need support, help, prayer, and so on. No, we are people forever needing help, forever inseparably bound to God and one another. Prayer is communication, a bid for connection with and support from God. Why would a relationship with substances suddenly create a line that doesn't otherwise exist? What if seeking help when we locate ourselves within the range of AUD could be as normal as prayer—a prayer for healing, just like what we'd offer for a friend headed into surgery? Or as normal as any other form of communication—a bid for support and connection from the spiritual communities that have vowed to be bound to us in love?

Unpredictable Paths

In *Beyond Addiction,* Jeffrey Foote and Carrie Wilkens explain different ways to view the process of healing our relationship with substances. It offers an alternative to the "tough love" approach—an alternative that involves promoting kindness, positive reinforcement, and motivational and behavioral strategies to help those who are struggling. Foote and Wilkens define "stages of change" as (1) precontemplation or not thinking about change, (2) contemplation or getting ready, (3) preparation or readiness, (4) action, and (5) maintenance.[2] The stages are a "process rather than an event": people can move in and out of these stages.[3] The text explains how a person exiting rehab is usually in the action stage, highly motivated by their experience of support. The ways we might support the person in the action stage not only would be unhelpful for someone in the precontemplation stage but would probably do more harm than good. It's vital that the way we care for people meets them in the stage they occupy, because otherwise it can hinder their healing.[4] *Beyond Addiction* offers a nonlinear framework for understanding change, with a reminder: "It is important to try to

2. Jeffrey Foote and Carrie Wilkens, *Beyond Addiction: How Science and Kindness Help People Change* (New York: Scribner, 2014), 70–72.

3. Foote and Wilkens, *Beyond Addiction,* 72.

4. Foote and Wilkens, *Beyond Addiction,* 72.

resist comparing your loved one's, or your own, pace and style of changing with others'. Preconceived notions of how the change process should go will only set you up for disappointment, as change seldom follows a predictable path."[5]

A spiritual community—of all places!—should be a place where we understand nonlinear healing. When I think about time and sobriety, I remember how I was taught I had to "start over" in fundamentalism through rededicating my life to Jesus Christ. When I became Episcopalian, my first thought was extremely Baptist: I should get rebaptized. I had been baptized only once, so I figured that in the grand scheme of things, only two baptisms was still a record low. But in the Episcopal Church we don't rebaptize, and at first it grieved me. I wanted to mark the change, to honor my new way of expressing my faith. But then I learned why we don't rebaptize: we believe God acted in our first baptism and will never leave or forsake us. We cannot go out of the grace of God, so we needn't try to reenter it. And I believe this same way of understanding God's faithfulness to us—a faithfulness completely devoid of morality and meritocracy—is pivotal in changing how we love people who struggle with alcohol. I never need to get rebaptized because nothing can remove me from the grace of God; in the same way, nothing can remove me from the path toward my healing.

Early in sobriety I was invited to a dinner with people I had shared drinks with, so they had a glass of wine waiting for me. I could tell nobody needed my short TED Talk about my sobriety, the root causes of addiction, and why this was an idea worth spreading. Plus, I sensed that telling my story

5. Foote and Wilkens, *Beyond Addiction*, 73.

would be more triggering for me than liberating. In the past when I had struggled with how to decline a drink, I had always caved and would end up drinking the way I always did. This time, when they offered me a glass of wine, I accepted. I carried it around with me, drinking a few sips. At one point they topped it off, but I didn't drink it any more that evening; I left a full glass of wine on the table when I left. To some, this would be cause to reset back to day one of my sobriety because I drank, but I don't agree. I wasn't carrying around a glass of wine because I wanted to drink; I was carrying around a glass of wine because I wanted to stay sober! It was easier for me to accept the drink, take a few sips, enjoy my evening without drawing attention to my resolve not to drink, then go home secure in the knowledge that I would wake up the next morning without a hangover. This experience didn't just help me stay sober, it solidified my desire to be sober. Y'all, I didn't want to drink the wine: it was a tool, not a temptation. There's no one-size-fits-all option for sobriety, but I needed the grace to accept a glass of wine in order to reject a return to drinking.

The Way the Father Waits

When I read the parable from Luke's Gospel about the prodigal son (15:11–32), I wonder if the real power of the passage is what Luke doesn't tell us—the way the father waits. I picture the father waking to find an empty bed where his son should have been, first hoping he had already gone out into the fields, then searching the grounds, scanning for the familiar features of his son's face. With each step he returns to all the fears of loss that have crossed his mind over the years. Each morning and each evening he scans the horizon, his eyes searching in a way we can only call prayer, begging that his hope is not in vain.

Then, one day, as he scans the horizon, he sees something off in the distance, and for a split second he wonders whether it is a mirage, but then he remembers: this is prayer. Even when the son is far off, he can tell just by his gait: this is my son. His hope was not in vain; what was lost is now found. The father begins to run. Finally, he is holding his son, squeezing him almost to the point of pain; the father trembles from the tears, from the way our arms begin to shake if we hold on to someone as if we might never let them go. The son launches into the words he has practiced the whole way home, the script he has fervently said to himself in hopes that it will save him from judgment and abandonment: "Father, I have si—" But his father is holding him so tightly it's hard to get words out; his mouth is caught in the shoulder of his father's tunic. He's trying to lift his head so he can speak: "I have sinned against heaven and—" But his father is crying, and the son can barely hear himself over the father's joyful tears.

The son is speaking but the father has started to yell over him, the father's voice breaking into that near-yodeling sound of relief. The father is asking for a robe to cover his son's tired body and is dressing his son in a way that reminds the boy of what he always was: worthy. The father is yelling for servants to prepare some food, overjoyed to hold his son but grieved to find the face he has searched for now so gaunt. The father is looking past the son, still calling out for the young man's care, and the son is trying to grab his father's face to get him to focus on the words he is uttering, because he hasn't finished his apology, but when his father does stop to look at him, he still talks over the son's words, muttering, "Thank God you are home."

Finally, the son raises his voice because he is hell-bent on saying the words he arrived to say. Right as he launches back into his apology, his father begins to speak as well. Like another Pentecost, they speak as one, saying: "I am no longer worthy to be called your son!" "This son of mine was dead and is alive again; he was lost and is found!" Their words fall over each other, becoming unintelligible. They make their way back to the home, where food and celebration await, and when they are almost there, the father stops to take his son's face in his hands. He stares into the face he has looked for night and day, and he rejoices that his son is found.

This is how God loves people who struggle with drugs. The father does not let the stigma of the son's choices serve as a barrier to the way he loves him. No, the father's love for the prodigal son looks like care for his well-being, a desperate search to be reunited with him, however he is when he returns. The father showers words of love and worthiness over his son to the point that he can barely even hear the son's confession, not because the son is wrong to confess but because the father has not spent these days waiting to get an apology—he has spent these days waiting to hold his son.

The older brother isn't as forgiving as the father. He learns of his prodigal brother's return, and he is furious—he has been obedient and dutiful, has never disobeyed his father, and works hard for the family. He's angry because his brother is wasteful and does things the family doesn't approve of—the sort of stuff the older brother never even tried because he thought it would get him kicked out. But the prodigal son isn't just not kicked out, he is celebrated for his return.

Transforming our hearts to be more compassionate to people who struggle with drugs will require us to release our inner older brother.

I often see the older-brother mentality projected onto people who have a problematic relationship with alcohol. It sounds like this:

- "Well, I've never gotten so drunk that I got myself in trouble; they need to drink less."
- "I'm a law-abiding citizen, and if a person breaks that law, they should expect to face the consequences."
- "They just need to get their lives together; stop asking for handouts."
- "They got themselves into this mess and they should have to get themselves out of it."

But this mentality is rebuked by the father, because the father hasn't been tallying offenses and waiting for a good-enough apology and a promise that the prodigal son will do better. The father has been waiting only to hold his son. When we allow stigma to overshadow grace, we miss the chance to experience the kind of grace that believes we—all of us—are worth the wait.

I know there is real brokenness in the world, that there are ways addiction has harmed us, and there are reasons why we can't just get out the finest robes and move on. No understanding of changing our relationship with alcohol can neglect the abuse that has come from the relationship. However, maybe we can begin to see how God loves people who struggle with drugs while we continue to seek healing for our abuse or trauma stemming from someone who struggles with drugs. As communities, we can carry some of the burden of this conflict, taking on the role of agents of grace. Our care for people struggling with drugs can be modeled after the searching and forgiving father, trusting in God's love for them while praying for the Spirit's illumination of the ways we are called to bear witness to how the dead are being brought back to life, the lost are being found.

If you have struggled in your drinking, you might relate to the prodigal son. You might feel even just one of his feelings—yearning for love and comfort, fearing what you will find in your bank account if you open it, needing to ask for support but wishing you felt more comfortable asking, as hungry for food as you are to experience the life you hoped for. Maybe you've heaped judgment upon yourself, convinced yourself you're not worthy to be loved. Maybe you feel lost. Maybe you've tried to come up with the right apology, choosing your words to make sure you express how much you hate yourself, how much you're going to try to do better, how much you know this is your fault.

If this is how you feel, try to remember how the father loves the son. We live in a world that makes you think you need to hate yourself just enough, you need to feel just unworthy enough, you need to have an apology that is sorry enough— but this way of understanding your struggle has everything to do with stigma and nothing to do with the Spirit. God hasn't been tallying your offenses and waiting for a good-enough apology and a promise that you will do better. God cares for your well-being, searches desperately to receive you however you are when you arrive, waits for you as a prayer, and holds you in hope, because hope does not disappoint. God showers words of love and worthiness over you, speaking through your confession with a love so booming it raises the dead to life, and you are the one being raised.

Yes, you likely have confessions you wish to make, regrets you've been harboring, an awareness of the mistakes you've made and the harm you've caused. On this side of death, we can't go back, and our pasts still require reckoning. But first, just let yourself be held. You can let go of guilt for a second, because it is good to release what you hold over yourself, to receive mercy, to remember we are more than the worst thing we have ever done.[6]

You will meet people who do not believe God could be this loving, people who don't recognize that you are just a human being and human beings need help, people who believe that you deserve what happened to you even though they know nothing about you, people who say that criminalizing you is how to heal you. And beloved, those people are not God, and I hope you will love yourself enough to remember you are loved in the same way that the father loves his prodigal boy.

We cannot go out of the grace of God, so there is no morality or meritocracy to separate us from God—and that includes our relationship with substances. God, like the father, certainly cares for our well-being and wishes we would feel good in mind, body, and soul. God's plea for us, as desperate as the father's search for his son, is that we would have an abundant and joyful life, but the mercy of God means we are worthy of this abundant life as we are now, however it is we are. If we slip up, the Spirit's only response is to shower words

6. Francesca Trianni and Carlos H. Martinelli, "Bryan Stevenson: 'Believe Things You Haven't Seen,'" *Time*, April 30, 2022, https://time.com/collection-post /3928285/bryan-stevenson-interview-time-100/.

of love and worthiness over us, because love and worthiness are the only words God has to say to us. We can stay inside the brave inkling calling us to change our drinking, knowing every movement into and out of drinking is a movement inside the love of God. You can rest inside this love instead of shaming yourself if you slip up, because every movement is a chance to receive the wisdom that will teach you how to cross the threshold into a party and, when you cross that threshold again, know you stayed inside your joy for the night.

refresh and reflect

If you drink, spend some time thinking about the way you drink. If any of the questions from the AUD assessment made you pause, stay in the pause even a moment longer than you want to. It's understandable to not want to engage the question, but the question doesn't hold bad news, only wisdom. After thinking about the way you drink, imagine the story of the prodigal son and place yourself in his shoes. In his shoes, follow his journey out of his home and then back into his father's arms. Receive the arms of the father's mercy and try to let yourself be held, even imagining his trembling arms holding you tight.

yet another day one

Healing Doesn't Have to Be Linear

I PICKED MY QUIT DAY months in advance, choosing to grieve alcohol like the companion it had become. I took my last "drinking vacation," and I knew, as I hung out with various friends leading up to the date that this way of being together was coming to an end. It was a quiet grief, but a grief held between God and myself, shared between my soul and the Spirit, who is always able to receive whatever grief we think we have to carry alone. My clients sometimes feel bad about how they keep wanting to drink, so I share this part of my story, because of course you are grieving when you say goodbye to alcohol. If we are going to change our relationship with alcohol, it's important to honor how we might feel as though the decision will leave a hole in our lives. It is a void: something has been removed, and we've been taught that the removal of alcohol might remove many of the tender and beautiful parts of our personalities and lives.

The morning of my quit day, I woke up and wrote, "November 11, 2018. Yet another day one." At the time, I wondered whether it would be a day one like all the others, as this was a promise to myself I had repeatedly broken; I couldn't have known that it would become my most recent day one, even after almost four years. Remember, we can be open not just to quitting cold turkey but to the long obedience in the same direction. Wherever we are—whether we are reading the Big Book with a box of chardonnay or celebrating years sober—can be a place of healing.

During the first three months of my sobriety, I navigated Thanksgiving, Christmas, an Episcopal conference, a vacation, an ordination, and my birthday. (FYI: these are all major accomplishments in sober life, each one more difficult than earning a master's degree, honestly.) When I went to my friend's ordination, I knew I could get a hotel and spend time with my friends. I was deep in the trenches of loneliness, so the idea of a hotel felt more enticing than ever, but I knew myself well enough to know I had a 3 percent chance of staying sober. I weighed all the pros and cons five times over, until I finally decided to drive there and back in one night—a five-hour round trip—because I wanted to see people I love, but I wanted to stay sober just the same. I got home, dead tired, close to one o'clock in the morning. (Sober bedtime is like 8:30 p.m., so this literally counts as one of the two miracles I need to officially become a saint.) The caffeine required to make the trip made me toss and turn, so on top of the exhaustion from driving, I slept terribly. I woke up the next morning bone tired—truly, my whole body was ready to meet Jesus—but I woke up sober. With the world's largest cup of coffee, I sat by the front window and thanked God, because I knew waking up bone tired was better than waking up hung over. This is what I mean when I say equal parts terror and amazement—the terror of going, but the amazement of loving myself enough to greet God with thanksgiving the morning after, with a bone-tired soul somehow fully awake to the Spirit. Every time I attended an event I didn't think I could survive sober, I like to say I strengthened my sober muscle. And boy did I get opportunities to strengthen that muscle in a short period of time.

But amid the strengthening, I didn't want to talk about it (and y'all, I am not short on words). I prayed, sincerely:

God,
I feel strongly that this could just be between you and me.
Thank you for your time.
   Regards,
   EJW
Sent from my iPhone

I am writing this book because God is not respecting my boundaries. I was fully dedicated to the private sober life until I was invited to preach at a clergy renewal-of-vows service. Between the invitation to preach and walking up into the cathedral pulpit, I learned that multiple priests I know and love were struggling with substances. My heart broke out of care for them, and inside the heartbreak, I was wrestling with the question central to my invitation to preach: What might God want me to say to a room full of clergy? I chose to preach about my sobriety—which happened to be the first time I had talked about it at all. Ascending the pulpit stairs at St. Paul's Cathedral in Oklahoma City, I vowed to follow the

Spirit's call to radically change the trajectory of my life and to bear witness from the sacred middle ground.

I posted the sermon on social media, then drove for about an hour and a half. I stopped for gas and couldn't believe the notifications (equal parts terror and amazement). I learned that my fear of talking about sobriety was apparently almost universal. I feared the judgment, the way people might talk about me after they got past the hand-shaking line following the service, the way they might suck in the air through their clenched teeth as if to say "yikes." But I'm not sure whether I feared their judgment, or my judgment, or both. The fear forced me to reckon with how I had reacted pre-sobriety when I heard about someone struggling. The judgment then, too, was an externalization of my wondering whether we were similar, but in a way that scared me.

Sharing publicly that I had quit drinking—given all the fears—went beautifully. As people began to reach out to ask for support or to tell me they were also sober, I felt even more supported in my choice. But I also faced the overwhelm of people asking for support. A ministry had awakened, and it wasn't in a church—it was in my direct messages. Through sharing, I had opened a world inside my vocation, and that cathedral vow asked me to change the course and shape of my life without much knowledge about what this new world would contain. It was terrifying, but it was accompanied by the peace of God that took up residence in the seat of my soul. The absence of alcohol created a space I didn't know the Spirit had filled, in the tabernacle of my heart where God wishes to dwell. As it always goes with joy, my palpable fear was met with confidence through faith in the God who came to dwell in my sober soul. God was calling me into a new vocation, the next part of my long obedience in the same direction.

When we think about our calling, it's natural to go straight to figuring out a job, but that can be a narrow understanding of how the heart and soul encourage us toward joy through understanding and pursuing our vocation (which may or may not be a job). It doesn't surprise me that a massive number of people are burned out, feel underappreciated at work, or struggle with rising costs and financial stress. So, even if we know our calling, the realities of our lives might make following it feel impossible, and this can become a reason to self-medicate with alcohol.

One of the most common patterns I see in coaching won't shock you: the immediate cocktail after work. The stress of the day, or the looming dread of going back tomorrow, creates a craving for escape. Enter the 5:00 p.m. booze. However, the more we use alcohol to take the edge off, the more we both supercharge the edge and train our brains to ask for the escape. Sure enough, we show up to work the next day and the work culture has not changed overnight. But now we are starting the day depleted of energy, so by the end of the day we are tired upon tired, seeking a way to unwind. In this pattern, we often aren't mindfully choosing a cocktail, lining it up against a long list of different ways we could release some stress at the close of the day. Instead, we are caught in a feedback loop or, for reasons outside our control, we don't feel we have tons of coping mechanisms at our disposal.

This is why coping with a job you hate by drinking can hurt you more than help you. The escape from overwhelm becomes an escape from how we might dream of better things, an escape from having a dream about anything at all, because the numbness disconnects us from the creativity, courage, and clarity that could help us forge a new path. When it comes to the soul, the depressive and anxiety-inducing side effects of alcohol can keep us in a job or other situation where we don't want to be. Sobriety is deeply interconnected to the human soul to the extent that abundant use of alcohol can disconnect us from the inklings that might otherwise give us positive direction in our prodigal wanderings.

Calling is not just a question of what you do with your life; it is also about whether you feel worthy of the hopes you have harbored in your soul. The effects of drinking on the mind, body, and soul can chip away at our worthiness by turning up the volume on negative self-talk and inhibiting us to the point that we make decisions we feel disqualify us from believing in ourselves. In their groundbreaking work *Motivational Interviewing: Preparing People to Change Addictive Behavior*, William R. Miller and Stephen Rollnick note that "sometimes the bolstering of self-esteem is a necessary prerequisite to motivation for change."[1] In the context of the workplace or communities where we are united by our vocations, it's not just about whether we find our work fulfilling; we are also influenced by whether we feel appreciated by the people in the workplace or vocational community with us. If you need to stay in an unfulfilling job in order to survive, you're not just disconnected from your calling—you're trapped in a system you hate. Even when we may want to change, lack of self-esteem can undermine the desire for change, keeping us inside the feedback loop we want to exit. Our lack of fulfillment in vocation—possibly due to disliking our day-to-day

1. William R. Miller and Stephen Rollnick, *Motivational Interviewing: Preparing People to Change Addictive Behavior* (New York: Guilford, 1992), 44.

tasks or feeling unappreciated by those in power—piles stress and discontent onto our lives. This stress naturally requires coping, but using alcohol to cope can hold us in patterns that work against our joy. Many can't change their means, because society has devalued people for reasons outside their control, so we must remember that this is communal, not individual, work. Healing is not just about me changing my relationship with alcohol; it's about getting out of these patterns to become more passionate about social change that provides everyone who wishes to heal with the tools to do so—because all people deserve fulfillment and joy.

A question I often get is this: How did you actually quit? Often people assume I went to Alcoholics Anonymous, but I didn't. Going to AA would have posed some practical challenges for me, because I was in rural Oklahoma and knew of only one meeting-place, which was housed in the church where I was the priest. If I was going to be able to look into this part of my life, it would have to be in a place that wasn't also my workplace. Also, AA has steps. My life is a graveyard of workbooks, journals, courses, bookmarked websites, and saved emails with life-changing ways to revolutionize this plane of existence, but I can only assume they are life-changing because I have not read any of them, because they all involve steps. I have assembled three pieces of furniture from IKEA in thirty-five years of life and believe I am joined to Job in our mutual sufferings. I have started *The Artist's Way* every three years for over a decade and never made it to an artist's date. How was I going to finish a program?

But my barriers weren't just practical. At the earliest-earliest-hadn't-changed-my-drinking-at-all stage, I would come home from a long day at work, fix dinner, and open up a box of wine and the Big Book at the same time. As I moved through its pages, I would read things that felt helpful, then read something that felt disconnected. Sometimes the language triggered my shame and I would set it down, not knowing what to make of it. I knew then, and still know, that AA saves lives. It has been a powerful way of healing for so many people. Still, I couldn't connect with the process, and it took years before I'd find other ways into my sober healing.

I didn't then, and don't now, identify as an alcoholic, which felt required in order to join AA. I have had traumatic experiences with people who self-identified as alcoholics, so the word feels connected to some of the trauma that exacerbated my drinking. Brené Brown talks about her own experience of not connecting with AA, which brought to mind her teaching on how guilt language says "I did something bad" while shame language says "I am bad." The way the Big Book hit me then made me feel as though I were bad, and I knew (even before I finally quit) that shame was part of my drinking, so it couldn't also be my way into healing from drinking. AA is a beautiful path; it's just not mine. I needed a way forward that would not send me toward the shame that was triggering my drinking; I needed a way forward that might make me trust in the radical idea I professed but hardly believed: that I was loved at all, but especially that I was loved by God.

As a recovery coach, I'm open with my clients about my nonlinear road to sobriety. I drank, tried to quit for like five hours, drank again, quit for maybe two days, drank again, did my Whole28—you get the idea. So how did I finally quit? Well, I had tried to quit a million times out of self-hatred. I'd wake up, look at my text messages, look at my bank account, remember something I said, realize there were things I said that I couldn't remember, and spiral into self-hatred, vowing not to drink anymore. As the day wore on, I'd somehow spiral further down, finally ending the day with a drink to escape the spiral. Shame will never lead us out of shame; shame will always send us toward another drink. My way forward was quitting not because I hated myself but because I finally loved myself; I finally believed I was worthy of the beautiful life I believed could be mine on the other side of sobriety. My path wasn't linear, but I stayed on it—and I'm still going.

The nonlinear path exists outside how some view recovery, but I encourage people to use whatever ways of healing feel most powerful for them. For instance, counting sober days isn't helpful for all people. When I meet with recovery coaching clients, I'm trying to learn what is motivational and demotivational for them. For some, seeing the count go up every day on a sober app might make them feel stronger in their pursuit of sobriety. However, for others, day counting can result in feeling that if they slip up, they have to start over, which can trigger a binge because they fall into the mentality that says, "Well, I've already messed up, so I might as well keep going." Either way, if our understanding of the path to healing brings up shame, it is counterintuitive to our hope, because shame only fuels our return to destructive patterns. This is why I tell clients that if they slip up, the most important next step is to care for themselves, because getting out of the feedback loop is part of reducing harm. I was finally able to quit because I was motivated by joy, not shame, which meant releasing self-punishment to receive the love of God and a newfound love for myself.

On November 11, 2018, when I wrote "yet another day one," I assumed that it would become just another day in a long line of day ones; I worried that there would be many more day ones to follow. But I am still sober. Even when we are teetering on the edge, not sure whether it has stuck—asking God, Google, and everyone else how to quit—we are quitting. I know now what I couldn't have known then: the way I quit was to quit, drink again, quit again, drink again, and quit again, discovering I loved God and myself along the way.

My "day count" started on November 11, 2018, but when I look back on all the quits and restarts, I can't ever say I relapsed, because I never went back to who I was before. I always moved forward, forever moving inside the grace of God that preceded and followed me. When I started engaging with sobriety as an act of radical self-love born out of belief in God's love, my faith deepened because I could rest in the knowledge that God and I both know my issues. And that's the gift, because I've run and I've returned. The way old friends take secrets to the grave, God's knowledge of my faults isn't intended to bring shame but to remind me that God will take my faults to the grave and then destroy the grave.

Sobriety, sober curiosity, changing how we drink individually and in our communities—all of this can be opened up, as a reminder of our existence inside love and worthiness, if we are willing to change how we think about the pursuit of healing. This involves recognizing many roads to recovery. I'm inviting you to understand recovery as openly and without judgment as you can, confessing your judgment when it inevitably rears its ugly head. Instead of assuming that people need to quit drinking because they are scared of rock bottom, what if we invited all people to put a finger on the pulse of their drinking? Tend to your soul with a curiosity about your life, what you want from it, and how it could be more abundant with a different relationship with alcohol.

If we start with judgment, strictness, or labeling, we risk hardening curious hearts when instead we could empower everyone to lean into curiosity. If we invite everyone into this mindfulness, we end the us-versus-them binary that stigmatizes those who have the courage to seek change. If we don't embrace compassion as the foundation of our care for people who struggle with drugs, we will make sobriety seem so difficult that some might stay in pain rather than take the chance to heal.

refresh and reflect

Pause to think about what changing your relationship with alcohol could look like. Reflect by asking yourself whether you have been taught that there is a definitive path for a person who doesn't like how they drink. If so, what does this path look like? Write out the different parts of this path.

Survey this path to recovery. Do any parts feel helpful for you? Do any parts feel restrictive?

Now, pull back and think about healing more broadly. Reflect by asking yourself how you have healed in the past. What did this path look like? Write out the different parts of this path.

Survey this path to healing. What parts felt most helpful for you? What parts, if any, felt restrictive?

Receive the wisdom offered from these different messages and experiences of healing.

sobriety as incarnation and resurrection

Reawakening to the Goodness of Our Bodies

AFTER QUITTING A FEW TIMES, I learned it can be a long process for the mind, body, and soul to release toxins. I'm not a wellness guru, and I hate how detoxing has been turned into a diet. That said, detoxing from actual toxins is real. And in order for you to feel the freedom of releasing toxins, the toxins have to actually leave your system, which means it takes time to feel the positive effects of being alcohol free. But even after just a week or so of sobriety, my body slowly awakened.

The most immediate way my body showed up to me anew was in the morning. When I finally experienced a good morning—a sober morning—I found mornings so radical I didn't know what to do with them. This is not a turn of phrase. I would get up and think, "OK, but what am I going to do with these extra hours?" I'm pretty sure my behavior was so unexpected that I startled my kitchen the first time I walked in so early. Over time, I became comfortable with the hours between waking and needing to do anything—filling them with prayer, meditation, coffee, reading, texting friends, tweeting nonsense, and meal planning. (I'm listing prayer and meditation first as more of an aspiration than a practice.) I've slept poorly and woken up late only a few times since quitting drinking, and every time I regret missing the sacred space of my mornings. I'm shocked I could ever come to miss a part of my life I formerly had but always took for granted. A burden in my sober life is how I struggle with the time I missed, the mornings I didn't spend inside peace and slow, the holy sites where I prayed with a numb heart, the experiences I took for granted.

But it wasn't just mornings. I went out to eat a few weeks into sobriety and ordered something I had ordered before, but this time I couldn't eat it because it was too salty. The next day I tried to eat something preseasoned and had the same reaction. Why was everything so salty? I'm a priest and writer, not a nutritionist, so don't email me about this, but I started to believe that maybe my taste buds were coming alive. Is it possible my whole body, all the way down to my taste buds, had been so consistently numb that I had been over-salting my life for a decade?

As I awakened to my body, each passing morning offering a hope and energy that felt like the Spirit I had always wanted to know better, I wondered whether maybe my body, not the chalice, was the tangible reminder of the pure love of God poured out in creation. What if the distance I felt from my body had run parallel to the distance I felt from God? What if all the images in the church about the body—the resurrected body of Jesus, the church as the Body of Christ, the way we're all inseparable parts of the one Body—were clues? I have come to believe I was actually made in Christ's image, and when I feel unable to connect with God in the ways I was taught, I try to remember that all I have to do is sit inside my skin. I can prayerfully behold the image of Christ in just myself. Getting sober or changing how we drink invites us into a tender time of seeing Christ in ourselves and acknowledging how we might actually have been called "good" when we were made. Trying to see how I bear the image of Christ has helped me see that if *I* can bear the image of Christ, certainly everyone else can too.

Sobriety rooted me in my incarnation, bringing to mind Athanasius's writing about how God was made manifest in a body "that we might receive the idea of the unseen Father," about how God "endured the insolence of men that we might inherit immortality."[1] Athanasius proclaims that God became what we are that we might become what God is.[2] Incarnation, like sacraments, makes earthly things eternal in the way it makes death a transformation, not an end. Our minds, bodies, and souls take on this incarnational shape because we are within this world but able to transcend it, the same way

1. Athanasius, "On the Incarnation of the Word," available at *New Advent*, January 2022, https://www.newadvent.org/fathers/2802.htm.
2. Athanasius, "#108: Athanasius on Christ," ed. and trans. A. Robertson, Stephen Tomkins, and Dan Graves, Christian History Institute, January 2022, https://christianhistoryinstitute.org/study/module/athanasius. I have paraphrased here to remove gendered language for God.

we are destined for death but headed toward resurrection. Like eternity, transformation does not wait entirely on the other side of death: inklings of eternity are present within this human life, because our lives—like Jesus—are formed to be fully human and fully divine.

Through mindfulness around alcohol, we can behold the mixture of earth and heaven in a way we might struggle to notice if we are numbed to the quiet and sensitive ways of the Spirit. We know we've encountered God when we meet the gift approaching like terror and amazement, when we've found ourselves lost in a wonder we've rarely let ourselves wander into, when we are in a state of unknowing that should trigger every one of our greatest fears but instead feels like peace. Sobriety changes us with wonder, terror, amazement, and peace, because it is one way we can encounter God.

Who Sinned?

In John 9, we receive one of the grossest healing stories in Scripture, and it's my favorite. The disciples and Jesus are walking and see a man born blind. The disciples, forever giving us a way to enter into the story, are like, "Rabbi, quick quesh, who sinned—him or his parents—that he was born blind?" And Jesus is like, "Babe, you're telling on yourself: this is not about sin. Don't you see how beautiful he is, right now? Stop looking for sin and start looking for healing."

Jesus then spits onto the ground and mixes it with dirt to make some sort of Jesus paste to wipe on the man's eyes. The man is told to go wash in the pool of Siloam, which means "sent," and he is said to have been healed of blindness. This text has been interpreted in ableist ways, but that misunderstanding is exactly at the heart of the question the disciples ask and why Jesus corrects them. I picture the man tracing the face of Jesus in his hands when they first meet because he wishes to see God. And I know Jesus saw the man as beautiful, that Jesus felt the man's hands trace his face and knew the blind man saw God with a level of faithfulness the disciples would never know. The disciples are trying to figure out the man's sin. But Jesus—fully human and fully divine—knows that their question is the only sin in the room.

Culturally, we have spent years trying to answer the disciples' question: Who sinned—this person or their parents— that they struggle with drugs? And babe, we are telling on ourselves. We have been so consumed with calling people who struggle "sinners" that we have neglected to realize that our judgments are the only sins in the room. Meanwhile, Jesus is wiping profane holiness over those who struggle, and the hurting are emerging from the pool of Siloam with a new way of looking into the world. We all have the chance to claim the holiness of earthly things like dirt and spit and to hold them in as high regard as we hold the chalice, because there is nothing more sacramental than rebuking the confines we have placed around where divinity might be found just to then reveal it in the last place we might expect: dirt, spit, the soul whose challenges we try to explain away with judgment.

If you are curious about trying to change your relationship with alcohol, take heart: this isn't about your sin—changing your relationship with alcohol feels like tracing the face of God. It won't look neat and tidy—it's dirt and spit, after all— but the profanity is worth the holiness when you emerge from the pool of Siloam.

Yet when you get out of the pool of Siloam, you become part of a literal investigation into whether Jesus was allowed to heal you with his Jesus paste. I wish this weren't the next step in the Gospel—it hits too close to home, making this Gospel a perfect look into how we misunderstand recovery. The man's neighbors grill him because he was healed on the Sabbath, which means that Jesus broke the Sabbath law. Then the man's parents are called to testify that he is in fact now not blind, and they add that their son is of age and can answer for himself. Then the formerly blind man is brought back in and—to bring this full circle—the whole conversation goes back to sin. Jesus is now called the sinner. But the formerly blind man learned something about sin when Jesus wiped mud and spit on his eyes, so he isn't about to play the "who sinned?" game again. He says, "I do not know whether he is a sinner. One thing I do know, that though I was blind, now I see" (John 9:25). He has learned to stop looking for sin and to start looking for healing.

And here's the deal: this is a neighbor issue. This passage shows the betrayal of the man's neighbors, the people close to him, his immediate community. Given the opportunity to honor his healing, they instead drag the man, his family, God, and just about everyone else into a trial about his healing because there's controversy around how he was healed. The challenges faced by people who are struggling and trying to heal their relationship with alcohol today are no less judged. One of the realities of this incarnational life is that there is no perfect way to heal, because mixing divinity with the human body is about as neat as mixing spit and dirt. The reality of humanity means we must be open to different ways of healing. Some of the saddest moments I have experienced in the recovery community are when I witness people in recovery judging other people in recovery because they don't like how another person has healed or where they are in the process. When we see someone healing and turn away from celebration to instead investigate perceived sin, we act in opposition to the healing work of the Spirit by becoming neighbors who do not love our neighbors as we love ourselves. And babe, if someone else's healing feels suspicious to us, we are telling on ourselves.

Incarnation

The Spirit invites us to be connected to our profane holiness through understanding ourselves as people needing healing and as stewards of our bodies, these gifts entrusted to our care. Mindless alcohol use often means we miss inklings of healing and awakening because our capacity to be attentive is lost in our coping. Mindless alcohol use can also mean we lose track of how to care for our minds, bodies, and souls, which then naturally means we expend energy on surviving our pains, with no energy left to give to the inklings. Our struggle with healing is rarely composed of isolated events or willful choices; this is a cycle our humanity makes us susceptible to, and the Spirit begs us to care for our minds, bodies, and souls, as acts of stewardship, so we can be healed.

The incarnation tells us that we can't separate the mind, body, and soul—an important reminder as we bring mindfulness into our relationship with alcohol. We can, however, turn to practices and rituals that bridge the gaps between mind, body, and soul. The book *Mindfulness-Based*

Relapse Prevention for Addictive Behaviors offers the Body Scan practice:

> In the context of relapse prevention, the practice of paying attention to physical experience can be especially valuable, because experiences of reactivity, cravings, and urges often manifest physically before the subsequent chain of thoughts or reactions. When in automatic pilot mode, we often lose contact with the immediate physical experience. Thus, coming back to physical sensations is a way of reconnecting with present experience and can be a first step in shifting from habitual, reactive behavior to making more mindful and skillful choices.[3]

We can introduce spiritual practices like body scans or even receive anointing with oil and healing prayers around our drinking. These can help us escape the autopilot mode and connect to mind, body, and soul, because "the path to divinity is through our humanity, not around it."[4]

Sobriety is not a problem, not a reason to search for someone's sin; no, the choice to change our relationship with alcohol is a revolution so connected to the incarnation that it is the physical embodiment of taking Mary at her word when she utters the Magnificat against all odds. Sobriety is the experience of a soul releasing numbness in favor of magnifying the Lord, our spirits rejoicing in God. It is the kind of humbling favor that means we might have been looked upon as lowly, but we know we are blessed, we know great things

---

3. Sarah Bowen et al., *Mindfulness-Based Relapse Prevention for Addictive Behaviors: A Clinician's Guide*, 2nd ed. (New York: Guilford, 2021), 41.

4. Kevin O'Brien, *The Ignatian Adventure: Experiencing the Spiritual Exercises of Saint Ignatius in Daily Life* (Chicago: Loyola, 2011), 200.

have been done for us, and we know the gift of holiness we receive in our profanity.

Those of us who try to embody this song of praise know how, even in our fear, we receive the mercy of knowing it is bad news before it is good news, terror wed to amazement. We have received the strength of the Spirit; maybe we felt scattered in the thoughts of our hearts, but that strength did not abandon us to ourselves even when we were ready to abandon ourselves. We know that the power we once gave to alcohol—individually, in our communities, and in our society—was an identity conflict that had to be dethroned in order for us to thrive in right relationship with the Spirit, because our power is not given to us through the world's power but through the power of God, who sees us when we feel lowly, who knows how we arrived to God hungry for good things, who loved us when we were rich in the world but empty in soul. Yet when we began to trace God's face with our hands, we were healed by the Spirit. We were made new: God removed the riches that did not give us richness in mind, body, and spirit, and we received the good things we had hoped for, even though they looked like bad news before they could ever look like good news.

Sobriety is a proclamation that we believe in the incarnation, the belief that God became human so that humans might be given profane holiness through deliverance from death. Bringing mindfulness into our relationship with alcohol is an act of faith, in God and in ourselves. Faith in ourselves means believing that the Spirit speaks to us through our minds, bodies, and souls, because God reveals God's self through creation, of which we are a part. Sobriety invites us into the mystery of how God could withhold from us every ounce of participation in divinity, but God doesn't. Instead, God beckons us to meet the Spirit in ourselves through the same mixture of holiness given to Jesus: the confusing wedding of humanity and divinity. This connection to God through creation is the Spirit blessing us with the earth, the foundation, out of which we can grow the empathy, compassion, and liberation we need to be of service to the other creatures of God. Sobriety is not for anyone in and of themselves; it is for the awakening of ourselves and all of creation.

Resurrection

This awakening takes the form not only of incarnation but also of resurrection. Many Christians believe in the embodied resurrection, that on the Last and Final Day we will be made whole inside our bodies within eternity. I've grown to love this belief the more I've learned spiritual wisdom from my body, now seeing how our embodied resurrection can be a resurrection in real time, a way of honoring God's creation while keeping us both outwardly in our bodies and inwardly in our souls.

To witness the power of resurrection, we must return to our incarnation, how our bodies are created to resurrect and heal. Your cells are forever replacing themselves at such a rapid rate that every ten or so years you basically have a whole new set of cells. Consider neuroplasticity, defined as "the ability of the nervous system to change its activity in response to intrinsic or extrinsic stimuli by reorganizing its structure, functions, or connections."[5] The studies of neuroplasticity and genetics and the introduction of new technology have done wonders

5. Pedro Mateos-Aparicio and Antonio Rodriguez Moreno, "The Impact of Studying Brain Plasticity," *Frontiers in Cellular Neuroscience* 13 (February 2019), https://doi.org/10.3389/fncel.2019.00066.

for how we understand addiction, allowing us to explore the neurobiological processes that illuminate how much biology and sociocultural factors make us vulnerable to addiction or resistant to it.[6] While the brain's adaptation can lead us to hold on to addictive patterns, that same plasticity can also help us heal from them. Ways we can use neuroplasticity to heal our relationship with alcohol include the following:

- psychotherapy, such as cognitive behavioral therapy
- support groups where we can receive empathy that motivates us to change our patterns
- coaching that encourages habit change and offers practical help with coping
- medication-assisted treatments to manage symptoms well enough to build the capacity to seek other forms of behavior change
- different combinations of healing modalities[7]

Additionally, it's no secret that long-term alcohol use can cause alcohol-related liver disease. Many who drink fear alcohol-related liver disease, but we are not without hope. The liver is highly capable of healing itself when it isn't filtering alcohol. When the liver filters alcohol, it stops the cell-regeneration cycle, which means it loses cells and begins to deteriorate. Quitting drinking allows the liver to retain the

6. Nora D. Volkow and Maureen Boyle, "Neuroscience of Addiction: Relevance to Prevention and Treatment," *American Journal of Psychiatry*, April 25, 2018, https://doi.org/10.1176/appi.ajp.2018.17101174.

7. Maria Mavrikaki, "Brain Plasticity in Drug Addiction: Burden and Benefit," Harvard Health Publishing, June 26, 2020, https://www.health.harvard.edu/blog/brain-plasticity-in-drug-addiction-burden-and-benefit-2020062620479.

cells it would have lost, so it can restart its natural process of regeneration. Some people are able, through quitting drinking, to repair the harm caused to their livers by alcohol. All of this is to say: your body is created for healing. The resurrection we experience when we change our relationship with alcohol is truly a resurrection of our minds, our bodies, and our souls, and it is yet again not something new, not a blank slate: this resurrection comes through returning to the ways God created us to experience joy and wholeness.

And it's not even that our bodies are just built for resurrection; they are also built for pleasure. When we drink heavily, we act in opposition to the natural ways our body was created to bring us joy through pleasure. Problematic drinking confuses our body's relationship with dopamine. By confusing the body's understanding of desire, we can end up searching out experiences that are not pleasurable and instead are harmful, because we've lost our connection to true pleasure. Daniel Lieberman and Michael Long explain,

> Drugs destroy the delicate balance that the brain needs to function normally. Drugs stimulate dopamine release no matter what kind of situation the user is in. That confuses the brain, and it begins to connect drug use to everything. After a while, the brain becomes convinced that drugs are the answer to all aspects of life. Feel like celebrating? Use drugs. Feeling sad? Use drugs. Hanging out with a friend? Use drugs. Feeling stressed, bored, relaxed, tense, angry, powerful, resentful, tired, energetic? Use drugs.[8]

8. Daniel Z. Lieberman and Michael E. Long, *The Molecule of More: How a Single Chemical in Your Brain Drives Love, Sex, and Creativity—and Will Determine the Fate of the Human Race* (Dallas: BenBella, 2018), 39.

It's ironic how heavy alcohol use is often thought of as participation in hedonism, the theory that pleasure is the highest good in human life, when in fact alcohol distorts our understanding of desire and pleasure so deeply that it drives us away from both. Sobriety could, in a sense, be understood as hedonism rightly ordered: I can testify to the immense pleasure I experience by not drinking.

Mindfulness around alcohol is a return to how God made us for joy. In my sobriety, I see my embodied resurrection not as a distant hope but as a current reality, a promise from God greeting me in the wake of the day. No, my body isn't perfect—I still have aches and pains, and there's always a little ding on my annual physical. (I keep telling my doctor I'm sober, so I, personally, am already resurrected by Jesus Christ, but she does not apologize or remove her comments in the patient portal.) Yes, my body still has challenges, but inside sobriety they feel less like moments of dying and more like reminders that my body has needs just as my soul does. I never want to diminish the realities of being in a body, because embodied challenges call us into grief, sorrow, pain, and hardship. However, sobriety has given me a way to be in relationship with the day-to-day life of my body, such that when inevitable pain rears its head, I can speak to it with a gentleness and reverence for my body, born out of the reminder I have received in sobriety: this skin is part of the creation God has called "good" and worthy of care.

Through drinking I was pushing down difficulties in my life because I didn't know how else to love myself. I was doing my best. And even if I had never gotten sober, I know God would have kept looking at me with the eyes of mercy that God has always had upon me and upon you, because God knows better than anyone else that we are just trying to survive. I thought that if the pains finally surfaced, they would emerge from the depths to catch me, to attack me, to consume me in death, so I drank to keep them at bay, to keep myself alive. But what I found when I got sober—when I awakened enough to let my life come up for air, when those pains finally caught me and made it to the surface of my heart—is that those pains came not to attack me but to teach me. In pushing down pain and trauma because I thought I wouldn't survive them if they lived at the surface of my life, I was actually pushing down the wisdom and healing I sought when I opened the bottle to escape. I thought I was drinking to survive, but my survival was found in no longer fearing my pains and instead receiving their wisdom—this is how I resurrected in sobriety.

When we think about resurrection, we might think of Christ exiting the tomb, in victory over death—and that is one facet of resurrection. But we would be wise to settle into the resurrections that are also about the tenderness of each day that unfolds before us, the unpromised gift of newness. These gentle resurrections are the facets of God we might overlook if we are numb to our own hearts, the vessels through which God might be trying to impart that tender waking into our lives and also into the greater life of the world.

By acknowledging that this is a search for profound soul healing, we can grow in compassion toward people (including ourselves) who are trying to change this part of their lives. If we hear that someone is seeking support regarding their drinking, we shouldn't be sucking in air past our teeth, wondering either aloud or silently, "How bad did it get?" No, it should bring us to tears with wonder, because this one—this beloved child of God—is not dead but risen. It should make us want to praise God out of overwhelming thanksgiving, because we have heard a miraculous healing story worth its place in any of the gospels.

To resurrect through sobriety or mindfulness around alcohol, however, is not to begin again. No, we find ourselves forever on that sacred middle ground, the place where life and death are no longer bound. It's a place of joy but also difficulty; it's a place of healing, but it also holds the wound. To be on this sacred ground isn't an escape, because sobriety is the antithesis of escape. Alcohol tells us to escape; sobriety reminds us that we have the power to bear witness from the middle place, that we can survive telling the truth, that we are worthy of a life outside the cycles of death we previously called living. My sobriety served as a resurrection because I left a way of living that was closer to death and began to exist in the world with a new mind and heart. Still, a story of resurrection in recovery is just like the stories of resurrection from the Bible: the bodies still stink, our lives are still tombs holding very real death, and even when the Spirit appears to us on the road, we don't immediately know we are with God.

If we are on this path to healing, we may be walking with the fears that come when we have hoped for eternity but instead have seen death. The idea of changing our relationship with alcohol contains many fears of loss: the fear that we'll lose our identity and personality, that we'll lose the friendships we've fostered over booze, that we'll lose the shoestring holding together our marriage, or even that it might feel impossible to go to church and be sober at the same time. These are understandable fears, but they might hold us in death when what we really yearn for out of our identities, friendships, marriages, and spiritual communities is a joy found only through death then resurrection.

Walking beside God

During my two-month stint of sobriety—after Whole28 and Lent, before I went back to drinking and then quit for good (I told y'all it was nonlinear)—I packed a box for Goodwill with the stuff in my home that flaunted how I was a booze girl: the napkins declaring it was "wine o'clock," the pint glasses from different breweries I couldn't remember, the wall hanging with a list of types of beers and a nonfunctional bottle opener, can sleeves telling lies like "starting my day off right." I gave away drinking as an identity; it was a sign that something bigger was happening, something even bigger than whether alcohol touched my lips. Even when I went back to drinking, I didn't introduce alcohol back into my home, except one bottle of fancy gin. It was given to me by a friend, and I would have felt bad throwing it away. I didn't want to drink it, but I also didn't want to be wasteful. I was conflicted because it was a sign of community, how I had been known, an artifice upon which I had placed my fears of abandonment related to sobriety. The voice forever keeping me in the bottle said, "This makes you a person they love; to lose it is to lose them."

On the day I moved, I placed that bottle directly in a dumpster, not because I wished to lose those relationships, but because I knew relationships worth my time have to be built on soul, not spirits. It was still grievous: the clink of glass, the bottle rupturing in garbage, the fear that I still, to this day, have to put at bay—that somehow I lost love when I lost self-hatred. But if fighting for love means holding on to self-hatred, it is no love for me. This was death praying for resurrection, the dumpster a tomb, spices laid on the rupture in garbage to tame the smell and recognize the decay. In resurrection, no love is lost when self-hatred is put to death, but the grief remains, the death is real, and we still must hang in the middle place where we can't know whether this is the death of love or the death of an illusion, whether this is the introduction of true life and true belovedness. I still think about how I spent the first two years of my sobriety in a home with a full bottle of gin and didn't take a single shot. Somewhere in my soul I knew there was nothing in it for me anymore, that my soul could not be found at the bottom of a bottle.

We might have to brave the fear of living inside our true identities; we might have to brave the fear of losing our old selves to welcome the new. Death might be worth how the resurrection leads us into identity, friendships, relationships, and spirituality imbued with abundant life. Like the disciples on the walk to Emmaus, the walk into mindfulness around alcohol is step by step. But in the seemingly quiet and mundane step-by-step movement, you will be walking beside the incarnate God who gives life to the dead. In sobriety, I walk beside the incarnate God who gives joy to those of us who thought we'd have to trade ourselves in order to love ourselves, because in losing my life, I found it. If you choose to go down this path of mindfulness, try to locate yourself on the road to Emmaus, in step with God, within the blessing of resurrection. If someone you know chooses to go down this path of mindfulness, resist a posture of pity and ask yourself the question Jesus asks in John 20:13: "Why are you weeping?" Celebrate, because you have witnessed resurrection; you have seen the power of God.

Through sobriety, I've come not just to ponder the mystery of the incarnation and resurrection but to believe that these mysteries of God are actively shaping my life. The Spirit reminds me, through this practice of staying inside my body and my soul, how my divinity and humanity are not opposed to each other but are wed to each other. Mindfulness around alcohol can resurrect you, and it can place you fully inside your incarnation, but you'll still have to literally navigate eating, talking, consoling, teaching, and enjoying the company of others as a person who is sober or who drinks differently. Incarnation requires that we take on the difficulty of being alive, and resurrection requires that we go through death, but we can do this inside a connection to the Spirit who promises it is good news.

refresh and reflect

Try a Body Scan practice. Find a space with the least amount of distraction possible, using tools like an ambient playlist or pillows to help ease distractions you can't avoid. Position your body in a way that feels comfortable for you but that will keep you attentive. (For example, you might not want to lie down because that could make you want to fall asleep, and you'll want to stay aware of your body for this practice. But sitting comfortably is just fine.)

First, draw attention to your breath. Try to notice how your chest rises and falls, how the air fills your gut and is then released. Then, starting at the top of your head, slowly bring attention to the different parts of your body. Focus on your head, shoulders, arms, fingers, chest, heart, back, gut, pelvis, thighs, knees, and toes. Let your attention stop on each part of your body. Pause for a few breaths and try to be aware of how each section feels. Is it tight? relaxed? in pain? itchy? aching? Just notice the sensations in the different parts of your body. When you are finished, bring your attention back to your center—often the heart or gut—and close with a few deep breaths.

sobriety as liberation

Honoring Black and LGBTQ Wisdom

MY CARE FOR LIBERATION took on a new form when it was no longer mediated by the numbing power of alcohol. I know I still have work to do because liberation is lifelong work, like sobriety and spirituality, but my capacity for mourning the effects of racism and hate grew in sobriety. Now I'm more sensitive to the joys and tragedies of life, which means I feel a deeper sense of grief when faced with the loss of life due to racism, homophobia, and other forms of hatred.

Sobriety takes on its consistent form: returning us to what we were made for—joy, yes, but also a more compassionate heart, with deeper grief for the hate that grieves the heart of God. Sobriety gave me a new determination to pursue joy for me and for everyone else, especially in a society attempting to withhold joy from some. I have courage through sobriety that I lacked before because I thought sobriety was impossible, but here I am, doing the impossible, such that very little feels impossible anymore. If we are going to cultivate courage, it must be extended toward the gospel's calling to seek out the oppressed, to love and advocate for them.

When I was drinking, my White privilege coupled with numbness made it such that I knew the gospel calling to renounce the sin of racism, but I lived in disobedience. This is one of the many ways alcohol participated in the identity conflict between my professed beliefs and how I lived my life. After the death of George Floyd, I saw a tweet reminding me not just to grieve Black death but to celebrate Black joy. It was a profound reminder of the salvation of God that doesn't just keep us alive but, instead, offers beloved people of God a life of thriving; it was a reminder that Black life doesn't just matter but deserves abundant life, joy, all the riches of this world and the next. As a White person in sobriety, releasing numbness meant more deeply feeling grief at the loss of Black lives; I began to more deeply receive the beauty of those lives as well. I'm more able to feel the weight of how racist hatred destroys life, and I'm letting the power of feeling it give birth to grief and rage. I pray that this grief and rage becomes how I participate in helping Black lives to thrive, because then the way I live would come into alignment with my professed beliefs.

Patients or Prisoners

Sobriety also awakened me to the many ways drug policy laws are built upon racism. As Maia Szalavitz writes in *Undoing Drugs,* "By the 1960s, illegal drugs had been firmly linked in the American mind with poor, Black, and brown criminals—and the stereotype of the 'addict' as a lazy, devious, and violent sociopath mapped perfectly on to the racist stereotypes many Whites held about those groups. With a compliant media, it was easy to blame violence and poverty on drugs—and not the socioeconomic circumstances that actually do lead people to problematic relationships with substances."[1] Views on drug use are a hotbed of hypocrisy, because often wealth and race decide whether a person is celebrated or demonized for their drug use. White mindless participation in drug use upholds systems that use drug policies as tools to criminalize non-White people. The numbing factor of drug use can then distance White people from action and advocacy.

If White people desire liberation for Black and other marginalized people, we must be aware of the difference between the consequences White people often face when they use drugs and the consequences Black, Indigenous, and people of color (BIPOC) often face when they use drugs. I believe as White people we must put our finger on the pulse of our drug use to notice how the distance alcohol provides becomes the distance between professed belief and faithful action, a disobedience to resisting the forces of death that are destroying the creatures of God, especially the lives that are at the greatest risk of death because they are targeted by our unjust system. Participation in the system plus numbing in order to avoid facing the evils of the system become two powerful ways alcohol serves to delay justice, and justice delayed is justice denied.

Research notes several barriers for BIPOC people who struggle with substances: multilayered internal challenges

1. Maia Szalavitz, *Undoing Drugs: The Untold Story of Harm Reduction and the Future of Addiction* (New York: Hachette, 2021), 72.

stemming from family relationships and cultural stigma; external barriers such as racism and socioeconomic challenges; and systemic issues such as poverty, law enforcement encounters, less access to healthcare, and institutional barriers.[2] The discrimination, stress, racism, and trauma experienced by BIPOC communities lead to greater risks of health challenges such as depression, post-traumatic stress disorder, anxiety, and a challenging relationship with substances. Black women are vulnerable to even greater risks and challenges with substances because of stress and trauma. Emily Einstein illuminates how the messaging of drugs in the 1960s still affects how we understand drugs today, stating, "There is a history of racial bias and discrimination around drug use in this country. Who is considered a 'patient' and who is considered a 'criminal' is a fraught societal issue that plays out in doctor's offices, emergency departments, hospitals, courtrooms, prisons, and beyond. Although statistics vary by drug type, overall, White and Black people do not significantly differ in their use of drugs, yet the legal consequences they face are often very different."[3]

This racism limits care to those who need healing, so if we notice that our privilege gives us power in this unjust system, we must get honest about our participation in it and seek to overthrow it for the sake of our belief. Christians receive Philippians, Ephesians, Colossians, and Philemon from Paul the prisoner and profess to follow a savior who was imprisoned

2. Malini Ghoshal, "Race and Addiction: How Bias and Stigma Affect Treatment Access and Outcomes," *PsyCom Pro*, November 17, 2021, https://pro.psycom.net/special_reports/bipoc-mental-health-awareness-racism-in-psychiatry/race-and-addiction-treatment-outcomes.

3. As quoted in Ghoshal, "Race and Addiction."

and then handed a death sentence, so any belief in Christian Scripture is a belief that we can receive the liberating word of God from people in prison. Jesus doesn't align himself with the imprisoned because he simply loves them in a general way. No, Jesus aligns himself with the imprisoned because he sat beside them in the cell and because they were beside him on the cross, as they were together given into death by the evils of an unjust system. So, too, are Christians called to be aligned with those who are imprisoned, because Scripture proclaims that the experiences of those souls are worth recording the same as Paul's. But we can't just listen to them; we must also work to let the prisoner go free. If we have privilege and are upholding structures that continue imprisonment, we betray our calling to be healers in the world, whether through how numbness helps us ignore our participation or how numbness makes us fearful of our own gospel. Our mindfulness around drugs must extend to noticing how a White person can escape prison while a person of color can perform the same action and end up behind bars, because every time our culture imprisons someone instead of offering them care, we lock up Jesus just the same.

Womanist Theology

Womanist theology has informed my sobriety; it stresses the beauty of the salvation of God while acknowledging that it cannot exist as only an ethereal idea. No, salvation must touch the ground, must become part of the holiness touching our incarnate life. Sobriety, in the same way, is a deeply incarnate experience of holiness, which keeps me in that long obedience in the same direction—and the place where I am going is for my nourishment and for the healing of all people. In *Making a Way Out of No Way*, Monica A. Coleman writes, "Womanist theologies add the goals of survival, quality of life, and wholeness to black theology's goals of liberation and justice. Womanist theologians analyze the oppressive aspects of society that prevent black women from having the quality of life and wholeness that God desires for them and for all of creation," later stressing that salvation must "focus on achieving life and liberation here in the land of the living."[4] If salvation is a here-and-now act, and our faith believes in it, we must act in the here and now so that Black and other non-White people receive liberation and justice in this lifetime that looks like survival, quality of life, and wholeness. This is especially connected to changing our relationship with alcohol, because a sober awakening offers the quality of life and wholeness God desires for us and for all creation, and if we receive that gift, then we should become advocates for ensuring that quality of life and wholeness are then offered to the rest of creation.

The womanist focus on healing for Black women connects directly with what we know about how racism affects people struggling with substances: Black women are the most vulnerable. When we relegate a group of people to the margins, we attempt to push them further away from healing modalities that might help them recover from a challenging relationship with substances. The overwhelming strength shown from the margins is a testament to how they will find healing no matter what, how they will make a way out of no way. But the extent to which racism fights against healing calls

4. Monica A. Coleman, *Making a Way Out of No Way: A Womanist Theology* (Minneapolis: Fortress, 2008), 11.

spiritual communities to become the spaces of healing that the world tries to withhold. Those of us with privilege are called to awaken from our numbness, to take on the mission of no longer perpetuating the structures that criminalize non-White drug use while making White drug use a status symbol. When we look into our relationship with alcohol through the lens of liberation, our healing can't be insular, our salvation can't stay ethereal; salvation through sobriety is incarnate, and we can become bearers of liberation with the goal of fighting for survival, quality of life, and wholeness for BIPOC beloved children of God.

Celebrating Diversity

Chaney Allen

The same way we are called not just to grieve Black death but also to celebrate Black joy, I want to celebrate a Black healing story I love—Chaney Allen's *I'm Black and I'm Sober: The Timeless Story of a Woman's Journey Back to Sanity*, which was the first autobiography written by an African American woman in recovery from alcoholism. It is no longer in print, which is a tremendous loss because Allen's wisdom deserves to be shared. She got sober in the late 1960s and her book was published in the late 1970s, which illuminates the incredible vulnerability and courage she showed in telling her story, a vulnerability and courage inspired by her desire to save lives through it, especially Black lives.

Allen notes the challenges of being Black in recovery, writing, "Usually our heavy drinking is done at night and on weekends—when AA and most alcoholism programs are closed. Certain people will not come to the ghetto to help us after the sun goes down. (Some don't come when the sun is shining!) Do you dig, Sisters and Brothers? There are liquor stores on almost every corner in our communities, not theirs. They are there for profit, which goes to other communities. Our people are getting sicker, while they (the owners) are getting richer."[5] She tells the full truth of her story, the difficulties and how she healed, never mincing words. She covers such a range of realities that are necessarily faced if we want to heal from alcohol, even calling out church hypocrisy toward people who struggle with alcohol. She tells the story of a man who came to church visibly drunk, writing, "One lady said, 'What a disgrace! I am so glad I am a child of God.' I looked her straight in the eyes and as arrogant as I could, I said, 'And he is too.' I walked away while her mouth hung open. I was remembering all the times their tongues were flapping about me when I was in the Hell on earth."[6]

Allen healed through Alcoholics Anonymous, in time becoming a sponsor, and she tells the story of being called away from church to care for people struggling with their drinking and the response she received. She writes, "I was often called from church, home, or wherever I was to help. One lady said to me Sunday, 'Honey, don't forget your church comes first.' I said, 'Too many of us Christians are quick to criticize a drunk or drug addict or anyone else who does something wrong. I feel, to be Christ-like is to help, so I will see you after I take care of this drunk.'"[7] She even illuminates the role advertising plays in our culture's toxic relationship with alcohol,

5. Chaney Allen, *I'm Black and I'm Sober: The Timeless Story of a Woman's Journey Back to Sanity* (Center City, MN: Hazelden, 1978), xv–xvi.
6. Allen, *I'm Black and I'm Sober*, 204.
7. Allen, *I'm Black and I'm Sober*, 204.

writing, "If someone dies, alcohol is served at the wake. If there is a wedding, alcohol is served abundantly. When we are sad we drink. When we are happy we drink! Our society says, 'Drink! Drink! Drink.' . . . Society positively recycles the alcoholic's dollars. Isn't this a mixed up society? Although no one obviously forces us to drink, we are not able to get away from alcohol completely. It is all around us."[8]

Close to the end of the book, Allen offers ways to reframe our thinking that she calls "thinking drunk/thinking sober."[9] The list contains eighty-seven ways to shift our thinking! She profoundly illuminates the misconceptions we have about sobriety and problematic drinking, many of which are also noted in my work. Here are some of the points she covers:

- the false notion that drinking gives us courage
- the illusion that sober people are boring and drinkers are fun
- our urge to differentiate between "drugs" and "alcohol" when alcohol is a drug
- the way we drink to cope but it doesn't help us heal
- the lie that drunkenness makes our parties more entertaining
- the way we like to build a fancy bar as a sign of status
- the truth that sobriety isn't shameful and is instead a way to exit shame
- the fact that alcohol does not help us sleep
- the ways alcohol exacerbates problems instead of helping with them

8. Allen, *I'm Black and I'm Sober*, 220.
9. Allen, *I'm Black and I'm Sober*, 223–35.

In addition, she discusses definitions of what constitutes drinking that is "OK" versus "dangerous," even though those binaries don't help us (e.g., weekend drinking is fine because you have to drink in the morning to have a problem, or people who have problems are daily drinkers). She even digs into how gender norms can shape our relationship with substances in an effort to help us remove those norms if they are barriers to our healing. *I'm Black and I'm Sober* is a work of Black art and joy.

Jean Swallow

If we're going to pursue liberation from the harm of alcohol, we must also look into the work of Jean Swallow, who penned what is (as I am writing this) one of few books available on lesbian recovery, titled *Out from Under: Sober Dykes and Our Friends*, published in 1983. This too is out of print but is another tremendous work of wisdom that deserves to be widely shared. Swallow is, like Allen, incredibly vulnerable and courageous in telling her story—with courage inspired by her desire to save lives, especially LGBTQ lives, through it. She's willing to name the threat facing her community, writing, "In the lesbian community, according to a study released last summer, the statistics are: 38% alcoholic, 30% problem drinkers. For a lesbian, those statistics mean you either are one, or you love one."[10] To bring that forward, in 2022 as many as 25 percent of the entire LGBTQ community reports moderate alcohol dependency, whereas the general population comes in at about 5–10 percent. Within the community, the highest rates of problematic drinking occur among bisexual

10. Jean E. Swallow, *Out from Under: Sober Dykes and Our Friends* (San Francisco: Spinsters/Aunt Lute, 1983), ix.

women, 25 percent of whom reported heavy drinking.[11] Swallow's conclusion continues to be true: if you are part of the LGBTQ community or if you love people who are LGBTQ, you either have a challenging relationship with alcohol or you love someone who has a challenging relationship with alcohol.

To this day, Swallow challenges those of us who claim to be progressive, spiritual, and formed by liberation when she writes,

> I have repeatedly heard talk, indeed have heard the gospel, that we must throw off the messages of the patriarchy if we are to be free. . . . What we must recognize is that substance abuse is part of the patriarchy. . . . It is every bit as much a lie as sexism, capitalism, classism, racism and homophobia. Substance abuse and abusive behavior depend, like all others, on denial and half-truth, on scarcity models, projection, and rationalization. They are the words of the patriarchy made life. Substance abuse and abusive behavior do not help us in dealing with patriarchal oppression either. In fact, they have the same effects on us: low self-esteem, anger, depression, hopelessness and loss of purpose.[12]

Swallow presents the image of rhododendrons as a way to understand liberation, writing, "If my lesbian community were clean and sober, I believe that is what we would look like: alive and growing despite everything and blooming in all our ways. And I believe it is possible, even in the stunted forest of this alcohol and drug-filled world."[13]

11. "LGBTQ Alcoholism," Alcohol Rehab Guide, March 1, 2022, https://www.alcoholrehabguide.org/resources/lgbtq-alcoholism/.
12. Swallow, *Out from Under*, x.
13. Swallow, *Out from Under*, xii.

The prophetic image Swallow presents for the lesbian community is the image of hope I have for spiritual communities. If spiritual communities were clean and sober, I believe we too would look like a rhododendron: alive and growing despite everything, and blooming in all our ways. Will we get clean and sober? I don't know, but I know mindfulness is the next step toward our joy, and I believe joy is possible, even in the stunted forest of this drug-filled world. *Out from Under: Sober Dykes and Our Friends* is a work of LGBTQ art and joy.

Giving Credit Where Credit Is Due

Encountering Allen's and Swallow's witnesses to the power and beauty of sobriety was profound, but one aspect of receiving their wisdom felt grievous: I felt as though I had heard it before, as though I had even said some of it before. I'm grateful for every witness to the power and beauty of sobriety I have received in sober spaces, because each has helped me heal and get to where I am today: offering my own witness to this power and beauty. The grief and guilt come when I realize that so much of the revolutionary sobriety wisdom I have received from White women, and then shared myself, was already expressed by a Black woman in 1978 and a lesbian woman in 1983. I'm not saying we shouldn't honor wisdom in whatever way we receive it—I needed to hear it in any way to get to today, and you are literally reading a book about sobriety by a White woman. However, if we are going to bear witness to liberation, we must receive this profound wisdom and credit how it comes to us through the courage to share something as vulnerable as a story of recovery. These prophetic witnesses to sobriety give us wisdom out of the margins; they told their stories knowing it might put them in danger, knowing it could have cost them their lives, but they believed that losing their lives for the sake of saving those who struggle was worth the risk.

If you're feeling moved by some of the insights in this book, please recognize how much of what I have said was first spoken by Allen and Swallow. The pain caused by alcohol is especially hard for Black and LGBTQ communities because of the injustices and harm they have already suffered. In order not to double down on harm against them, we must interrogate the wisdom we receive so we can honor where it came from, knowing the likelihood that we will find it comes out of Black and LGBTQ art and joy. The invitation into mindfulness around alcohol includes recognizing how Black and LGBTQ wisdom has invited us into our joy and facilitated our healing, and how we must practice gratitude for this joy and healing by overturning the systems attempting to withhold joy and healing from them. Wisdom appropriated may not be intentional, but we must honor the impact of appropriation regardless.

Becoming Bearers of Liberation

For spiritual communities to bear witness to resurrection, we must be bearers of liberation, participating in creating a world with less injustice giving us reasons to understandably cope. Alcohol, through how it distances us from action and how it is used to uphold racist policies, acts in opposition to liberation, specifically liberation from harm toward BIPOC and LGBTQ people. Alcohol fuels our oppressive class structure, which offers freedom to the rich and imprisonment to the poor. These oppressions become even more dire when they are layered, because harm can be multiplied tenfold for people who find themselves with multiple identity points weaponized against them by our unjust society.

There are many meaningful and important entry points to becoming bearers of liberation. For people with identity points that give them privilege (White, straight, cis, wealthy), becoming mindful can provide the first step toward becoming a bearer of liberation. Some actions that can be taken include the following:

- acknowledging how we sit in relationship to drugs
- recognizing how those who are different from us sit in relationship to drugs by receiving their stories and wisdom
- asking how our mindlessness toward this difference has been an act of privilege and how it has caused harm
- changing our relationship with alcohol and becoming empathetic toward those who struggle
- seeking to end oppressive policies and practices that try to withhold healing from beloved children of God

We must not associate ourselves with the powers and principalities of this world that seek to kill or imprison someone for using drugs, sometimes even for using the same drugs we use, but must instead associate ourselves with the power of God, which proclaims that what the world calls powerless and criminal is what God called Son. Our mindfulness around alcohol can awaken us to God and ourselves, but this awakening to God will then send us down that long unfolding process of liberation, because it will call us to better love the people God loves. We don't just change our relationship with alcohol for ourselves, we change because we believe in what the world could look like if the whole of creation knew the beauty of liberation—even in the stunted forest of this drug-filled world.

If we, as spiritual communities and people, claim to believe in the liberation of BIPOC and LGBTQ communities, we must honor their recovery wisdom by both increasing healing opportunities for marginalized people and ending oppressive policies that criminalize pain for some who seek healing. In order to profess our faith in salvation with integrity, we must take the advice of womanist theology and make the goals of survival, quality of life, and wholeness for Black life more important to us than the ways we uphold privilege. We must place importance on the survival, quality of life, and wholeness of LGBTQ life through celebrating the beauty of who they are so that they are not encouraged to numb out of their identities, identities that are professions of beauty, proof of how God perfectly makes us. If our faith claims to worship a God who grieves the destruction of the creatures of God, then we must name our sins of commission and omission, especially when we have been negligent in caring for BIPOC and LGBTQ lives—sins that are transgressions against our profession of faith.

If we are people of privilege and acknowledge our transgressions of faith, we can begin the process of repentance, which is a passageway into joy. Repentance, returning to God and to one another, requires us to become allies and advocates for those who not only have struggled with substances but have been led into lives that demand coping because of our negligence. We must confess how our idolatry of alcohol has exacerbated the oppression we are called to overthrow, but the beauty of this repentance is that it comes bearing liberation, and liberation begets liberation, so this forgiveness reconciles us to God, to ourselves, and to the world.

Even just the movement into a closer practice of what we believe can remove some of the spiritual tension and, in losing the tension, we can find the joy of knowing the beauty of freedom. This is a movement of the Spirit to help us down the path out of participation in oppression and into participation in the joy that is equal parts terror and amazement. We can find hope in the fruits of the Spirit that must be waiting for us, regardless of where we sit in relationship to these challenges deserving liberation: maybe we will be invited into ways of healing that society has tried to withhold from us, maybe our faith will come into alignment with our actions and we will resolve our spiritual identity crisis, or maybe we will receive the absolution of God that is resurrection. Across all peoples, we can receive the joy that comes if we bear witness to the Spirit's liberating work in a world desperate for a truth that stands a chance of setting the captive free.

refresh and reflect

Let's think about how we can become better agents for liberation. Ask yourself (1) how you have witnessed society withholding survival, quality of life, and wholeness from marginalized people and communities and (2) how you think this withholding has affected people struggling with substances.

Close your eyes and imagine a world where survival, quality of life, and wholeness are offered to Black, LGBTQ, and other marginalized people. Move through your community and neighboring communities, seeing with your mind's eye. What joy do you notice? How is this image different from your community and neighboring communities right now?

sobriety as discernment

Practices That Remind Us of Our Belovedness

I RECOGNIZE WHY you might feel overwhelmed by the idea of changing a culture of drinking and our presence within it, and how this work might seem challenging—or impossible. Yes, changing our relationship with alcohol requires a look at life that is varied, ranging from internal work to the external systems at play, all the way down to the extremely practical questions of how to physically enter the party and then leave the party sober—or just with your integrity intact. Before you go too far into being incapacitated, come back to center. The invitation to mindfulness around alcohol is a calling to take seriously the trauma alcohol causes and to choose to bear witness to the harm, whether it's the way we've been harmed, the way we've participated in harm, or both. Bearing witness is not a cry for prohibiting or demonizing drug use. It is, instead, a calling to cultivate a noticing heart, and to show up to your relationship with alcohol with noticing and care as your intent. Mindfulness around alcohol is a request to gather the vulnerability and courage needed for the journey into your sacred middle ground, where you will occupy the gap between your death and your life. Let yourself be in the sacred middle and bear witness to the part of your drinking left unprocessed, knowing that you are accompanied by self-forgiveness, acceptance, and self-compassion as your balm.

People often ask me, "How do I help someone I know who is struggling?" and I always give the same answer: The best way to help your friend who is struggling is to first bring mindfulness into your own relationship with alcohol. Come to your own awareness of your alcohol use; cultivate a heart of noticing toward yourself first; guard your heart with self-forgiveness, acceptance, and self-compassion; start down your own healing journey. Here's why helping has to start by going inward: if we go down this path, the way we will show up for others will be different, because we have cultivated a wellspring out of which we can draw water to quench our thirst and pour a glass of zero-proof refreshment for someone else. You'll notice that I don't say "get sober" to those who ask; rather, I invite them to bear witness to the harm they have survived. In doing so, they will begin the greater process of bearing witness to the harm others are surviving, which is at the heart of healing our relationship with alcohol personally and communally.

The choice to bear witness—to our harm and the harm we grieve in a loved one's life—becomes how we gather up the disparate parts of our souls, how we begin to walk behind our loved ones to gather up a few of their fragments too, to then give ourselves as a burnt offering on the altar of joy. If we ask them to join us where we are, we increase the chance that they will know we aren't sending them to a place we've never been, we aren't condemning them to the idea that they "have a problem." If we invite them to where we already are, they will know we wish to be with them, that we want to be close to them; we bear witness to our shared harm and exist together in the middle space of healing.

Often I will have back-to-back appointments with spiritual directees and recovery coaching clients, and while they share a foundation of self-forgiveness, acceptance, and self-compassion, the loci of spiritual direction and recovery coaching are quite different. In spiritual direction, the hope is to build an altar where the directee can place the cares sitting at the front of their soul. Spiritual direction receives the offering and holds space for its joy, grief, hope, and questions. I ask questions like this: How is your soul today? We lay down our curiosities and burdens, trusting that the Spirit will be our mediator and advocate. I close our time with prayer, acting as an intercessor, gathering the directee's petitions as my own offering on the altar.

After a quick bathroom break, I show up to a recovery coaching call, which has a very different vibe. I'm still holding space for the complexities, still honoring the questions, still in many ways building the altar, and because of who I am as a person, I'm always curious about everyone's soul. But in coaching, the focus is on my client's relationship with alcohol. We're looking into the past week for clues about how that's going, observing patterns and triggers, trying to locate how shame might be connected to their drinking, noticing how other more subconscious triggers might be at play. Then, at the close, we set goals for the next week, because weekly goal-setting encourages habit change. I'm very clear with my clients about a few things: (1) There is no such thing as failing at a goal. If they set a goal and struggle to achieve it, there is wisdom to receive, and we can learn from it to help them heal. (2) They set their goals. If specific goals don't come to mind for them, I suggest goals based on what we have uncovered during the session, but ultimately they lead the way in their healing. (3) Goals have to be achievable, because achievable goals are motivational: they help us see our progress. If goals aren't achievable, they become demotivational.

As I invite you into a practice of mindfulness around alcohol, remember it's a practice of blending spiritual direction and recovery coaching, because it requires the shared foundation of self-forgiveness, acceptance, and self-compassion—and upon that altar we will need to honor the questions, the emotions, and the requests made of God, all while tending to the state of our souls. It's also a practice of looking into our relationship with alcohol, observing patterns and triggers, locating how shame is at work, and setting practical goals based on the wisdom uncovered, because that is how we can bear witness to the harm of alcohol and begin to heal it, in ourselves and in our communities.

Harm Reduction

I believe in blending discernment practices and harm reduction principles, which results in a way of healing that encourages you to be less concerned with external declarations of what is the "right way" and more focused on locating where you are in your relationship with alcohol, bringing attention to that relationship, and charting a course toward changing your relationship with alcohol in any way. The use of discernment practices (holy listening) connects you to the wisdom of your mind, body, and soul, allowing your wisdom, the cultivation of self-trust, and shame resilience to become the key tools in your healing. This fluidity around healing is born out of the principles for harm reduction, as I believe harm reduction connects to the spiritual teachings of loving ourselves and others as we are in this moment, being honest about ourselves and the realities around us, being open to the many ways God brings healing into the world, and releasing certainty in favor of trust.

If you are new to the principles of harm reduction, they offer a wide array of strategies to help people who use drugs reduce their harm. Common harm reduction strategies include "safer use, managed use, abstinence, meeting people who use drugs 'where they're at,' and addressing conditions of use along with the use itself."[1] The shape of harm reduction provides a spirit of fluidity around healing that influences my own spirit of bringing discernment into healing, because harm reduction honors many paths to changing our relationship with drugs.

The National Harm Reduction Coalition offers a list of principles to give the work of harm reduction its guiding focus (see the accompanying sidebar).

Harm reduction seeks to honor each individual where they are, wherever it is that they are, which is a way of understanding healing reminiscent of how Jesus's ministry was a

1. "Principles of Harm Reduction," National Harm Reduction Coalition, 2020, https://harmreduction.org/about-us/principles-of-harm-reduction/.

Principles of Harm Reduction

1. Accepts, for better or worse, that licit and illicit drug use is part of our world and chooses to work to minimize its harmful effects rather than simply ignore or condemn them.
2. Understands drug use as a complex, multi-faceted phenomenon that encompasses a continuum of behaviors from severe use to total abstinence, and acknowledges that some ways of using drugs are clearly safer than others.
3. Establishes quality of individual and community life and well-being—not necessarily cessation of all drug use—as the criteria for successful interventions and policies.
4. Calls for the non-judgmental, non-coercive provision of services and resources to people who use drugs and the communities in which they live in order to assist them in reducing attendant harm.
5. Ensures that people who use drugs and those with a history of drug use routinely have a real voice in the creation of programs and policies designed to serve them.
6. Affirms people who use drugs (PWUD) themselves as the primary agents of reducing the harms of their drug use and seeks to empower PWUD to share information and support each other in strategies which meet their actual conditions of use.
7. Recognizes that the realities of poverty, class, racism, social isolation, past trauma, sex-based discrimination, and other social inequalities affect both people's vulnerability to and capacity for effectively dealing with drug-related harm.
8. Does not attempt to minimize or ignore the real and tragic harm and danger that can be associated with illicit drug use.

Source: "Principles of Harm Reduction," National Harm Reduction Coalition, 2020, https://harmreduction.org/about-us/principles-of-harm-reduction/.

ministry of interruption. People stopped him as he was walking through the crowd—he literally met people where they were, as they were. Jesus encountered people who needed healing and, instead of interrogating them, asking whether they'd quit, or telling them to get it together, he had compassion for them. Jesus could look at just about anyone in any state and see how they—as they were in that moment—had faith and possibility, and how their faith made them well. Harm reduction understands that people who use drugs deserve to be received in compassion, deserve to be met wherever they are, deserve for their faith and possibility to be recognized, and deserve to be made well. And, if you drink alcohol, you are one of these very people, and you are deserving of this as well.

If we wish to heal our relationship with alcohol while honoring the state of our soul, we can bring harm reduction principles into our context personally and communally, bearing witness to the harm to try to reduce it. Here are eight practical steps inspired by harm reduction principles. As you read through them, think about how they could be applied to your personal life and the life of your community.

First, bear witness to the truth of drugs and their harm, regardless of their legality, and honor this truth by avoiding ignorance or demonization of people who use drugs. Choose to build a spiritual foundation of healing through acceptance, compassion, and empathy. Break down the dividing wall between "people who drink" and "drug users," because alcohol is a drug.

Second, acknowledge drug use as a complex, multifaceted phenomenon, reminding yourself and others how alcohol use disorder is on a range and healing will need to honor this range. Recognize how some ways of using drugs are safer than others, but be mindful of the bias toward assuming that alcohol is safer than other drugs, because it isn't. In 2020, almost 92,000 people died from drug-involved overdose of "illicit" drugs (cocaine, heroin, meth) or prescription opioids: a grievous loss of life.[2] Our society tends to think that these "illicit" drugs are more dangerous and considers alcohol a safer and more socially acceptable form of drug use, but in 2020, alcohol-related deaths rose to 99,017, which disproves this notion.[3] We must honor a range of healing, recognize that safe drug use is better than unsafe drug use, and confront our culture's bias toward alcohol.

Third, bear the word of salvation, the kind that improves the quality of life and well-being for individuals and communities, first for the marginalized, then extending to all. Remember that we each bear the image of God and are called "good" regardless of our drug use. Let salvation be our guide, embracing fluidity of care over policies and judgments. Prioritize care for helping our world heal from the trauma and fatality of alcohol, especially when you think about how to use the time and energy of your community.

Fourth, discern how bearing the word of salvation calls for providing nonjudgmental, noncoercive services and resources for people who use drugs, and pray with your community about how you can be a source of healing. The opportunities are varied: your community space could host an organization offering harm reduction services, you could

2. "Overdose Death Rates," National Institute on Drug Abuse, January 20, 2022, https://nida.nih.gov/drug-topics/trends-statistics/overdose-death-rates.

3. Roni Caryn Rabin, "Alcohol-Related Deaths Spiked during the Pandemic, a Study Shows," *New York Times*, March 22, 2022, https://www.nytimes.com/2022/03/22/health/alcohol-deaths-covid.html.

partner with local harm reduction groups doing this work, or you could write letters to elected officials requesting that more services be made available to provide help to afflicted populations. You could let these principles become how you preach and teach about healing the trauma caused by alcohol.

Fifth, remember that people who use drugs are worthy of having influence over the shape of their lives and the shape of their communities, including yours. Share their wisdom, and wisdom about ways to respond to the global health crisis of alcohol, in your programs and with your leadership. Teach and lead from a place of compassion toward people who use drugs.

Sixth, make sure your community affirms the dignity of every human being, including people who use drugs, and becomes a place where they know, above anything else, that you love them and support them in finding the way of healing that works for them. Empower them in their search for healing and trust them to be the primary agent of reducing the harms of their drug use. Addiction is a search for healing. Honor how this crisis is a spiritual ache; a desire to find wholeness in mind, body, and soul; and ask how your spiritual practices can support people as they heal.

Seventh, when you bear witness to the truth about alcohol, bear witness to the full truth, including how poverty, class, racism, social isolation, past trauma, sex-based discrimination, and other social inequalities mean we don't just have experiences of harm due to alcohol but instead often end up in a state of harm caused by alcohol. Protect the dignity of every human being through acknowledging how these factors affect a person's vulnerability to and capacity for managing their relationship with alcohol, instead of suggesting that their struggle is a moral failure. Commit to action against societal evils as a way of supporting those who struggle with drugs because of these realities.

And finally, refuse to minimize or ignore the profoundly grievous danger and death caused by alcohol. Every community has people who are struggling with alcohol, so every community must grieve the harm and danger it causes. Commit to changing your norms around alcohol, starting with how you have events, how you talk about the drug, how you make jokes about alcohol, and how you might link identity to drug use, either positively or negatively.

Coming Home to Ourselves

If harm reduction principles shape our discernment, we can be led by the Spirit into the heart of this work—the internal work, the communal work, the willingness to open ourselves up to life in the sacred middle—which brings joy. We have joy in us, the joy that is our birthright, and healing from the state of trauma caused by alcohol offers a level of attention and care for yourself, and others, through which your joy may be made complete. You cannot accept the invitation to mindfulness around alcohol without the inevitability of change, and change is terrifying—hence, this is a joy of equal parts terror and amazement. But every encounter with the proclamation of bad news before there is good news changes the trajectory of not just the recipients of the news but also of the whole of creation, and we desperately need the Spirit to change our trajectory so that we may turn away from our destruction and toward our joy.

This movement leads us into the wide array of beauty I see in my recovery coaching clients when they awaken to the

Spirit and themselves through healing their relationship with alcohol. I bear witness to people becoming mindful of their drinking, their shame and pain, and the connections within all of it, but they do so with the opportunity to process the event of the drinking and its aftermath. Often they experience noticeable changes in their anxiety and depression, as well as decreased disruption in their lives because they have reduced harm and the intrusive and distressing memories of drinking. Intrusive and distressing memories of drinking never go away, but when my clients experience them, they have care practices to respond with and a space to receive love if they slip up.

Changing how we drink can lead us into epiphanies about ourselves, our relationships, and our futures, because the reduction of anxiety, depression, and disruption can provide a greater capacity for hope. As we begin to heal from the trauma of alcohol, there is still a sense of exhaustion accompanying the process, but the energy is given toward healing, which helps us exit cycles of harm. Energy is still necessary for protection and survival, but, over time, we often find that protection and survival can begin to find an origin in self-forgiveness, acceptance, and self-compassion, which participates in the greater work of healing. Healing from alcohol is a lifelong process, but the choice to reside in the sacred middle place is a choice to, slowly but surely, move out of cycles of harm caused by alcohol and into joy.

When we come home to ourselves through healing, we return to the moment God called us "good" and "beloved," the primary identity we might have forgotten along the way. So many of us have awakened to the Spirit and ourselves through sobriety or mindfulness around alcohol, and I have witnessed our lives change, because in releasing our numbness, we have received our joy. Joy calls us into an awareness of the callings we had long accidentally numbed, the collateral damage of understandably numbing our pain. In coming home to ourselves, we have to assess what we are coming home to, and not in an ethereal sense but in a practical one. Receiving this joy can change our relationships, our jobs, where we live, how we spend our time, what we believe—because the Spirit changes us at the root of who we are, and naturally this new birth ripples into the rest of our lives. This rippling is change, and change can feel devastating, but it's bad news becoming good news—the terror we endure in order to experience the amazement of our miraculous birth. This grand returning to our belovedness needs spiritual practices, because we must learn to remember our belovedness in the face of triggers.

My course, Discerning Sobriety, shares Ignatian wisdom to guide us through sober discernment with a question to anchor us: Where is the movement (of the Spirit) coming from, and where is it leading me?[4] Here are just a few practices you can try to orient yourself around the question as you come home to yourself.

Examen

The Ignatian practice of praying the Examen is a prayerful way to review the day and its events, challenges, and joys. By bringing attention to the whole of our days, we can notice how alcohol affects us, whether we are in a challenging

4. Kevin O'Brien, *The Ignatian Adventure: Experiencing the Spiritual Exercises of Saint Ignatius in Daily Life* (Chicago: Loyola, 2011), 118.

pattern with drinking or whether we have changed how we drink. This attention to the day helps us notice alcohol's effects on our stressors, joys, and callings, and its effects on the state of our soul. The Examen follows this form:

- Become aware of God's presence.
- Review the day with gratitude.
- Pay attention to your emotions.
- Choose one feature of the day and pray from it.
- Look forward to tomorrow.[5]

Self-Care

I hate talking about self-care, because much of what we see now as "self-care" finds its origin in capitalism, part of a lucrative industry profiting off our culture of exhaustion, and I'm not here to promote it. However, true practices of caring for yourself (which can always be low-cost or no-cost!) are integral to healing in mind, body, and soul. I can't tell you what self-care is for you, because it needs to honor your unique self, so I encourage you to try a few things and see what sticks.

Here are some ways to generate self-care ideas: What feels like a deep breath after you've struggled to take one? What's something you keep saying you'd like to try but never do because it isn't prioritized? What's the least sexy thing you could do to make your life a little easier today? (If you can find a sexy way to meal plan, please contact me immediately.) Think about these questions and make a list of true self-care practices, because when we're struggling, we are rarely able

5. "The Daily Examen," IgnatianSpirituality.com, September 2022, https://www.ignatianspirituality.com/ignatian-prayer/the-examen/.

to think with the most creative part of our brains. Some examples include scheduling "appointments" between God and yourself on your calendar; finding small ways to reduce stress during the week (using frozen meals, getting home products to make daily tasks a little bit easier, putting a few bills on auto-draft if you can afford it); choosing a bath over a quick shower; or seeing whether you can take a five-minute break during the day for a cup of tea. Think about small things that can help you pause and engage joy, and try not to minimize the importance of "small" practices because they all add up, and any self-care act is better than none.

Self-Talk

During my first attempt at sobriety, I received daily positive affirmation essays and rolled my eyes so hard you could hear it. I had done the whole Brené Brown thing; I am literally certified in her work, but self-talk felt impossible. I gritted my teeth and read positive statements every morning, until one day I made a mistake and, instead of verbally cursing myself out, I returned to the affirmation from the day. I'm not saying I never speak poorly to myself (again, it's a lifelong process), but the rate at which I cuss myself out has dropped dramatically. Write out one or two positive statements you can say to yourself each morning: a line of Scripture, a song lyric, a short quotation—you name it. You might also listen attentively for what your shame voice says to you and write an affirmation to refute it. For instance, Shame Voice says, "You drink too much; no wonder your partner left." (Sorry, I went for the jugular because sobriety is like that.) Your affirmation might be to say, "I am worthy of love and belonging as I am. I am allowed to heal." Refuting shame voices is vital in healing our relationship with alcohol, because shame keeps us in the cycles of numbing we are trying to change.

Before anybody says it: refuting shame talk doesn't mean condoning all your behavior. We are invited into confession and repentance when we do wrong, but our actions never determine our belovedness, and telling ourselves falsehoods about our worth only encourages self-harm—it never helps us reduce it.

Telling the Truth

The trick here is to tell the full truth, which means not getting caught up in romanticizing booze or spiraling into self-hatred. Telling the truth in this sense includes two steps: telling the truth about alcohol and telling the truth about your belovedness. Telling the truth about alcohol means using your imagination to play a drinking experience out to its true end before you drink. If you get a craving to drink or an invitation to go out drinking, you can turn to this practice. Imagine yourself going to the event or coming home from work, whatever scenario is tempting or triggering. Imagine drinking the first drink, as we are wont to do, but keep imagining: imagine the second, the third, however it tends to go for you. Imagine how you go to bed and how you wake up. Imagine what your tomorrow will feel like, what your body will feel like. Imagine opening your texts and your bank account, or looking into the eyes of your partner (if you have one). Once you've fully imagined the scenario, try to make your decision about whether you'll drink, how much, and so forth with this in mind.

This is a fuller truth of our relationship with alcohol than we tend to see in a craving, and it can help us make the decision in front of us from a place of mindfulness. You might get to the end of the practice and feel fine, which is great, but you also might feel some shame popping up. That's why the second part of the process is so vital: telling the truth about your belovedness. If we spiral into self-hatred, we will tell ourselves a lie more dangerous than romanticizing alcohol: the lie that we are not loveable. So return to your belovedness, because it is the full truth too.

Using These Practices in Community

These practices are possible first steps in a lifelong process, but it is a lifelong process forever relevant to loving yourself and others. While these practices focus on personal internal work, they can be translated into spiritual practices within your community:

Examen. Pray the Examen with your community, focusing on how you are called to bear witness to the harm caused by alcohol. For instance, instead of choosing one feature of the day and praying from it, you could let that space be occupied by asking God to lead you in sober discernment as a community.

Community-Care. Assess whether your community has a culture of rest or overwhelm so that you can address overwhelm and protect rest, because we know that overwhelm becomes a reason we need to cope and that self-care is a vital part of healthy coping skills.

Community-Talk. Pay attention to the messaging in your spiritual community (which includes what is said among leadership, from the pulpit, and elsewhere), and ask whether it is an affirming voice or a shame voice. If you can locate shame voices, write affirmations to refute them and let the affirmations shape community practice.

Telling the Truth. Tell the full truth about your community's relationship with alcohol without romanticizing booze or spiraling into self-hatred. Name the truth about your community's norms regarding alcohol, and tell the truth about your community's belovedness.

We know there is no such thing as a community untouched by the harm of alcohol, so there is no better time than this present moment to take our place on that sacred middle ground, to bear witness—looking across at each other, not down on each other. If you want to change your relationship with alcohol, individually or communally, you don't have to know what it will end up looking like in your life. We actually can't know what any part of our lives will look like, so this isn't a deviation from how we are but the truth of what it means to be alive. You can, however, listen to your mind, body, and soul. You can be vulnerable and courageous enough to face the truth of your drinking history, or the drinking history of your community, and compassionately begin to uncover the narratives guiding you. You can trust that where you are, and where you end up, is where you are meant to be.

You Can Do This

If you want to change your relationship with alcohol, you can change it, and there doesn't have to be an agenda or someone pushing you toward a decision to moderate or never drink again. You can begin to heal by just taking the question—how do I want to be in a relationship with alcohol?—up on its invitation to lead you into the sacred middle ground of joy, where you will get to know yourself and the Spirit with a deeper knowledge. You might begin to feel as if this is going nowhere good, whether because of opposition from loved ones or from others around you or because of the sheer difficulty of walking into a party and leaving it without drinking more than you intended. Remember: it's bad news before it's good news; it's an angel saying "fear not!" before it's a miraculous birth.

Christ shows up in humble skin, but his life is dedicated to healing. He is present to people in a way they've never known before; he knows things about them no one else could know; he greets strangers like old friends, because he knows his humanity as well as he knows his divinity. If we renounce our ambivalence to the trauma of alcohol and bear witness from the middle, the true presence of Christ—the fullness of divinity and humanity—can invite us into our own fullness. We are souls in humble skin, but through the power of incarnation and resurrection we can be present to ourselves and others in a new way, beholding people with a heart of clarity that isn't numbed by alcohol. We can arrive to strangers like old friends, because we can bravely exist inside minds and souls that are no longer narrowed by the anxiety alcohol forced on our weary bones.

We will always wrestle with the human part of us, because humble skin holds pain and death that can't be ignored any more than the harm of alcohol can be ignored. But the wrestling is part of the fullness of ourselves, not outside it, and if sobriety has taught me anything, it is this: I am able to survive the wrestling because God saw me while I was far off, after having searched the horizon for my face. God is joined to me in how we share the knowledge of my sins and the knowledge of the Spirit's grace. Every day I awake to God rushing to me, robing me in mercy, holding me with a trembling love, as I am gaunt but being led into a true banquet feast. From the second I asked the question, the second I wondered whether sobriety could bring me into the joy I yearned to receive, Jesus began mixing up spit and dirt to remind me of my holiness and my profanity, and in my struggle and in my healing, I am tracing God's face in my hands.

I resurrected as privately as I resurrected publicly. I got sober quietly in my home, but like a battering ram against the doors of the world, willing them to open for me the way I chose to open to God and to myself. I resurrected by way of my incarnation and resurrection and processed the long-unresolved harm in my life. In sobriety, I bear witness from the sacred middle ground, which is the island forever rescuing me from my inward sea. And on this island there is an altar of joy, where I make the offering of my life, the altar around which I now preside. Sobriety stands guard for me, my angel with the flaming sword, and nothing makes it to the altar of my joy unless it has the mark of my inner authority, born out of how I now listen to the Spirit. Sobriety is how I honor my mind, body, and soul, such that nothing is placed upon the altar of my joy unless it be part of the fluid area of my consent.

Sobriety is my crucial link with the Eternal, and it can be yours too.

refresh and reflect

This chapter offers many possible ways for you to continue the work of bringing mindfulness into your relationship with alcohol. You might even feel overwhelmed by the prospect of doing this internal and communal work. To help with overwhelm, just pick one of the following practices from the chapter to begin: praying the Examen, practicing small acts of self-care, paying attention to messaging, or telling the truth. Allow this one practice to be your anchor, trusting that when it's time to add another practice, you will know.

recommended resources

Sobriety and Sober Curiosity

Allen, Chaney. *I'm Black and I'm Sober: The Timeless Story of a Woman's Journey Back to Sanity*. Center City, MN: Hazelden, 1978.

Bowen, Sarah, Neha Chawla, Joel Grow, and G. Alan Marlatt. *Mindfulness-Based Relapse Prevention for Addictive Behaviors: A Clinician's Guide*. 2nd ed. New York: Guilford, 2021.

Grace, Annie. *This Naked Mind: Control Alcohol, Find Freedom, Discover Happiness and Change Your Life*. New York: Avery, 2018.

Gray, Catherine. *The Unexpected Joy of Being Sober: Discovering a Happy, Healthy, Wealthy Alcohol-Free Life*. London: Octopus, 2018.

Swallow, Jean E. *Out from Under: Sober Dykes and Our Friends*. San Francisco: Spinsters/Aunt Lute, 1983.

Szalavitz, Maia. *Undoing Drugs: The Untold Story of Harm Reduction and the Future of Addiction*. New York: Hachette, 2021.

Warrington, Ruby. *Sober Curious: The Blissful Sleep, Greater Focus, Limitless Presence, and Deep Connection Awaiting Us All on the Other Side of Alcohol*. New York: HarperOne, 2020.

Caring for Mind and Body

Brown, Brené. *Braving the Wilderness: The Quest for True Belonging and the Courage to Stand Alone.* New York: Random House, 2017.

Cherney, Kristeen. "Alcohol and Anxiety." Healthline, September 26, 2019. https://www.healthline.com/health/alcohol-and -anxiety.

DiLonardo, Mary Jo. "What Is Alcohol Withdrawal?" WebMD, November 26, 2021. https://www.webmd.com/mental-health /addiction/alcohol-withdrawal-symptoms-treatments#1.

Kuria, Mary W., David M. Ndetei, Isodore S. Obot, Lincoln I. Khasakhala, Betty M. Bagaka, Margaret N. Mbugua, and Judy Kamau. "The Association between Alcohol Dependence and Depression before and after Treatment for Alcohol Dependence." *ISRN Psychiatry,* January 26, 2012. https://www.ncbi .nlm.nih.gov/pmc/articles/PMC3658562/.

Lieberman, Daniel Z., and Michael E. Long. *The Molecule of More: How a Single Chemical in Your Brain Drives Love, Sex, and Creativity—and Will Determine the Fate of the Human Race.* Dallas: BenBella, 2018.

National Institute on Alcohol Abuse and Alcoholism. "Alcohol Use Disorder: A Comparison between DSM–IV and DSM–5." April 2021. https://www.niaaa.nih.gov/publications/brochures -and-fact-sheets/alcohol-use-disorder-comparison-between -dsm.

Smith, Joshua P., and Carrie L. Randall. "Anxiety and Alcohol Use Disorders." *Alcohol Research: Current Reviews* 34, no. 4 (2012): 414–31. https://www.ncbi.nlm.nih.gov/pmc/articles /PMC3860396/.

Tawwab, Nedra Glover. *Set Boundaries, Find Peace: A Guide to Reclaiming Yourself.* New York: TarcherPerigee, 2021.

World Health Organization. "Alcohol." July 2021. https://www.who .int/health-topics/alcohol#tab=tab_1.

World Health Organization. "Global Status Report on Alcohol and Health 2018." September 27, 2018. https://www.who.int/publi cations/i/item/9789241565639.

Spirituality

Coleman, Monica A. *Making a Way Out of No Way: A Womanist Theology.* Minneapolis: Fortress, 2008.

O'Brien, Kevin. *The Ignatian Adventure: Experiencing the Spiritual Exercises of Saint Ignatius in Daily Life.* Chicago: Loyola, 2011.

Peters, David W. *Post-Traumatic God: How the Church Cares for People Who Have Been to Hell and Back.* New York: Church Publishing, 2016.

Rambo, Shelly. *Spirit and Trauma: A Theology of Remaining.* Louisville: Westminster John Knox, 2010.

Thurman, Howard. *Meditations of the Heart.* Boston: Beacon, 1999.

Williams, Rowan. *Resurrection: Interpreting the Easter Gospel.* Cleveland: Pilgrim Press, 2003.

Changing Relationships with Alcohol

Clear, James. *Atomic Habits: An Easy and Proven Way to Build Good Habits and Break Bad Ones.* New York: Avery, 2018.

Foote, Jeffrey, and Carrie Wilkens. *Beyond Addiction: How Science and Kindness Help People Change.* New York: Scribner, 2014.

HAMS: Harm Reduction for Alcohol. https://hams.cc/.

Najavits, Lisa M. *Recovery from Trauma, Addiction, or Both: Strategies for Finding Your Best Self.* New York: Guilford, 2017.

National Harm Reduction Coalition. "Principles of Harm Reduction." 2020. https://harmreduction.org/about-us/principles-of-harm-reduction/.

Warde, Erin Jean. "Discerning Sobriety: The Course." 2021. https://www.erinjeanwarde.com/.

Erin Jean Warde (MDiv, Seminary of the Southwest) is an ordained Episcopal priest, spiritual director, sobriety coach, and speaker who lives in Austin, Texas. She offers a course (Discerning Sobriety), Substack community, and podcast. She is also a founding editor and editor at large of *Earth & Altar* and has written for *Mockingbird*, the *Christian Century*, and *Grow Christians*.